DON DADA

DON DADA

Assessing the Socio-economic and Political Power of Jamaica's Mafia Bosses

Damion Keith Blake

The University of the West Indies Press

Mona • St Augustine • Cave Hill • Global • Five Islands

First published in Jamaica, 2024 by
The University of the West Indies Press
7A Gibraltar Hall Road,
The UWI, Mona Campus,
Kingston 7, Jamaica
www.uwipress.com

© 2024, Damion Keith Blake
ISBN: 978-976-640-893-0 (Paperback)
       978-976-640-895-4 (Epub)

**A catalogue record of this book is available from
the National Library of Jamaica.**

Cover and Book Design by Christina Moore Fuller

Printed and Bound in the United States of America

To my mother Marcia Williams-Blake
(in memoriam) and the people of
Brown Villa, Kingston, Jamaica

Contents

List of Figures and Tables

Preface

In May 2010, the Jamaican government used its military and police arms of the state to capture, arrest and extradite Christopher 'Dudus' Coke to the United States on drug trafficking charges. Coke was Jamaica's last mega don. He derived this status from his considerable political influence, financial wealth and the para-military prowess accorded to him from leading the infamous 'Showa Posse' gang.

The Jamaican don is a violent non-state actor who wields considerable power and control inside the nation's garrison communities. A don is a male figure, usually from the community in which he plays a leadership role. Garrisons in Jamaica have often emerged as neighbourhoods that are don-ruled shadow versions of the official state. These are poor inner-city communities characterised by homogeneous, and in some cases, over-voting patterns for one of Jamaica's two major political parties: The People's National Party (PNP) or the Jamaica Labour Party (JLP). This book explores the major roles dons play in Jamaican garrisons. It focuses on a cluster of communities in the downtown metro area of Kingston, Jamaica. Additionally, it investigates the factors that account for the evolution of such roles performed by dons from the 1960s to the present. I used governance theories and the concept of embeddedness as an analytic framework to interpret the power and authority dons have in garrisons.

Dons, as it turned out, perform four central roles in garrisons: security/protection, social welfare, partisan mobilisation and law, order and conflict resolution via "jungle justice" measures. Different types of dons perform alternate mixes of these roles. The community case studies described here led me to develop a taxonomy of these informal community leaders by separating them into mega, area and street dons. I argue overall that dons are embedded governing authorities in Jamaican garrisons based on the socio-economic and political roles they carry out. By examining the responsibilities of dons in Jamaica, this analysis contributes to the literature on the activities of non-state criminal actors and their forms of influence on governance processes. The study suggests that it may now be appropriate to re-think the nature of governance and the actors we broadly assume are illegitimate holders of power and authority in developing nation contexts. It ends with suggestions on how to dissolve the power of dons and their gangs in Jamaica's inner-city communities.

Acknowledgements

I wish to acknowledge and thank the Social Science Research Council (SSRC) and the Open Society Foundation (OS) for awarding me a Drugs, Security and Democracy fellowship. The research fellowship allowed me to conduct seven months of field research in Jamaica. I am grateful also to the many Jamaicans who assisted me in obtaining and scheduling interviews; their support was invaluable.

ONE

Don Dada: Despots of Jamaica's Garrison Spaces

Introduction

The term "don dada" was popularised within Jamaica's dancehall musical space and culture in the 1990s. It is symbolic of someone who has the highest rank, often in an organised crime syndicate, is powerful, has financial prowess, is violent and above all, a person who is respected and feared. The Urban Dictionary describes a don dada as "someone who scared someone without saying anything. A don dada is someone you know not to mess with".[1] The Jamaican Patwah (Patois and Slang) Dictionary defines a don dada as, "the general, a bad man, the don of all dons, the highest-ranking boss in any activity, the most respected".[2] William Anthony Maragh, popularly known by his dancehall stage name, Super Cat, had a 1992 hit song "Don Dada". The lyrics graphically describe the bravado, respect, status and fear a don dada has in Jamaica. It also sums up the dynamic of urban inner-city life, the power of the gun and the power dons possess.

In simple terms, a don dada is a type of don, a criminal mafia boss in Jamaica, whose emergence and evolution are best understood within the context of the country's political history, its economy, and the impact of illicit transnational flows across the Americas. Narcotics (cocaine and marijuana) moving through the Caribbean Corridor into the United States (US) and the United Kingdom (UK) served to financially empower Jamaican dons. Simultaneously, the trafficking of guns and other small arms from the US into Jamaica gave dons and their gangs enormous "fire power" (Blake 2013 and 2020; Campbell 2020). The genealogy of the term "don" has European connections and as Rattary (2001) explains:

The word *"Don"* is of Spanish origin (1523). It is from the Latin 'dominus', which means master or lord. When prefixed to the Christian name, it becomes a title for a Spanish nobleman, gentleman, and a person of consequence, or university professor. We, however, are more familiar with the term as it refers to an Italian Mafia boss, a respected, powerful leader in that (originally) Sicilian secret criminal society.

These men are informal community leaders who typically have partisan ties, have benefited financially from the narcotics trade across the Americas and, on occasion, have used the material wealth they acquired thereby to provide socio-economic services to residents in garrison communities.[3] A don has significant power in these communities because of his command of a gang, access and willingness to use guns and violence as a means of creating fear and maintaining respect. Dons perform roles within their communities or "areas of control", which often accredits them with the named title of "area leader" and/or "community leader" (Campbell 2020; Leslie 2010).

The don is viewed as the consummate male, the "real big man";[4] he controls his gang and several women, has financial power, and demonstrates physical violence and prowess as a marker of his hegemonic position. Many Jamaican boys are acculturated to the use of force and to the perceived significance of exercising control over the home to "become men" (Chevannes 2002). The use of force and violence against women and other men are also features of the male masculinisation process in other Latin American and Caribbean countries. Jamaican boys can go onto the streets and the "corner" to interact with other boys and men who are considered dominant in their communities, while girls are expected to stay inside the home. On the streets and in the "yards"[5] of Jamaican garrisons, young boys and men learn social codes of bravado and machismo. This background of masculinity and gender is important to attaining a full understanding of who dons are, the status they have in garrisons and the roles they perform in such communities. There are different categories of dons in Jamaica, the don dada is the chief among dons, what I term the mega don. Later in the book, a taxonomy of don types is provided and an analysis of the divergent roles they perform.

Garrison Politics and Dons

Since its independence in 1962, Jamaica has not had a reversal or collapse of its democracy. Governments have been formed with political parties transitioning in and out of power without any attempts at a coup. Electoral victories and defeats are respected and accepted (Blake 2004; Powell and Lewis 2011). However, its democracy has been dogged by rampant police and political corruption, gang violence, organised crime and economic variability. The country's political history reveals an unholy union between elected officials and dons who operate as de facto despots of garrison communities (Leslie 2010).

Garrison spaces in Jamaica are sites where marginalised citizens reside. They first emerged as manufactured partisan politicised community spaces, controlled initially by demagogues of either of Jamaica's two main political parties-the Jamaica Labour Party (JLP) or the People's National Party (PNP). Later, with the official and unofficial patronage of either political party, garrisons evolved into don-ruled shadow versions of the official state (Arias 2017; Blake 2013). They are shanty inner-city communities characterised by homogeneous and, in some cases, patterns of over-voting[6] for either the PNP or the JLP. Garrisons are further characterised by governmental neglect, infrastructural decay and economic malaise. Many residents in these communities live below the poverty line and exist on the margins of Jamaican society (Campbell 2020). These ghettoes, in the classic sense of that term, often experience violence related to gang turf rivalries, partisan warfare, extra-judicial killings by the police – Jamaican Constabulary Force (JCF) – and contests concerning the dominance or relative status of a don or multiple dons (Munroe and Blake 2017).

Figueroa (1996) has argued that Jamaican garrisons are "totalitarian space[s]" overseen by dons, also referred to as "area leaders" or "strong men". This work, however, distinguishes between an area leader, or strong man and a don. Garrison residents view dons as evolving from area leaders. It is important to see these as overlapping categories as in some communities, residents accept the don as an area leader.[7] Chapter three explores the similarities and differences between Jamaican garrisons and other urban slum communities in Latin America. The partisan "roots" of garrisons are a distinguishing feature that sets Jamaican urban slum communities apart from other similar neighbourhoods in the Americas.

A report from the *National Committee on Political Tribalism* (The Kerr Report 1996), identified the garrison as a political as well as socio-cultural problem in Jamaica. The Committee's report concluded, "The most dysfunctional manifestation of the process of political tribalism has been the development of the garrison within constituencies (5)." It noted further, "a garrison, as the name suggests, is a political stronghold, a veritable fortress completely controlled by a party" (Kerr Report 1996, 5). Garrisons are politically manufactured communities that arose from:

- The development of housing districts (in the 1960s and 1970s) by different governments in Jamaica to secure party support;
- The homogenisation of voting patterns by pushing out opposition (minority) party supporters. Gang leaders (sometimes dons) under the orders of political officials; cleansed communities of residents that did not support the party of the elected representative for that neighbourhood;
- The ongoing use of strong-arm tactics and violence to secure a solid block of votes for one party in a particular community.

During the first decade of independence, elected representatives used dons as agents of political enforcement and mass mobilisation inside garrison communities (Sives 2002; Stone 1980). By the 1980s, however, the roles dons performed in their neighbourhoods changed and expanded beyond the realm of partisan politics. Their power evolved over time and the functions dons perform in garrisons are symptomatic of a diminished state capacity of successive Jamaican governments to maintain their centralised authority and legitimacy.

Don Dada pulls on extensive fieldwork, over the span of seven months, conducted inside several garrison communities that fall within political constituencies in the parishes of Kingston and St Andrew. Jamaican dons, of all ranks and types, use garrison communities as the headquarters for their criminal enterprises. Interestingly, they also have residences in these communities where they and/or their families live. Aside from their political characteristics, garrisons are also socio-cultural spaces that reflect some of the macro cultural and social mores of Jamaican society. Dancehall music and street dances, for example, are cultural products that originated and evolved from the urban poor and working classes in these inner-city communities (Cooper 2004; Hope 2006). Dons tend to insert and embed themselves within the socio-cultural fabric of garrisons; this affords them assent among residents. As the book argues, to understand the social power of Jamaican dons, the geo-political and social space of the garrison community must be explored.

Violence and Drugs Across the Americas

Historically, violence in the Latin American and Caribbean (LAC) region is associated with the legacies of colonialism, the Cold War, military coups, revolutions, guerrilla warfare, civil wars, and battles for independence (Pereira and Davis 2000; Warmington-Granston and Blake 2020). Violence across the region intensified by the 1980s into the 1990s as the trafficking of cocaine and marijuana from South America through the Caribbean corridor into the United States increased. Homicides, gun violence, gang turf wars, and organised criminality expanded as a result of this transnational enterprise (Willis 2017). The International Narcotics Control Board (INCB 2015), notes that "the region of Central America and the Caribbean continues to be used as a major transhipment area of consignments of drugs originating in South America and destined for North America and Europe" (49).

Since the end of the Cold War, the region has increasingly become criminalised and violent. Anthony Harriott (2008) contends that the Caribbean region has a 'subculture of violence' that manifests itself in its high murder rates, strong gang cultures, and prevalence of organised crime. Crime and homicide data within the region support his claim. The United Nations Office on Drugs and Crime (UNODC) 2019 report, *Global Study on Homicide,* notes that in 2017, the Americas region had 37.4 per cent of global homicide deaths, Africa had 35.1 per cent, Asia 22.5 per cent and Europe had 4.7 per cent. Dalby and Carranza (2018) in an Insight Crime report pointed out that the most dangerous countries in the Americas region on account of homicides were Venezuela (89 per 100,000), El Salvador (60 per 100,000), Jamaica (55.7 per 100,000), Honduras (42.8 per 100,000), and Brazil (29.7 per

Figure 1.1: Trend of Homicides in Jamaica 2001–2022

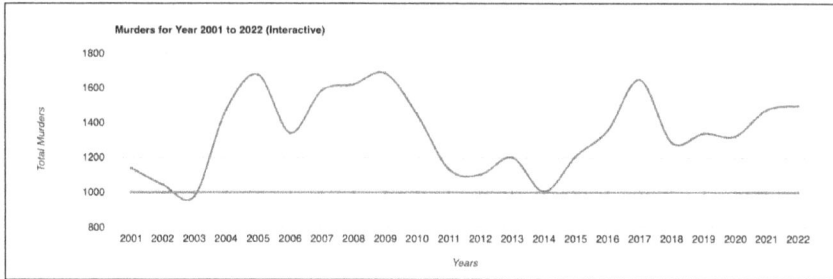

Source: *Jamaica Constabulary Force website at https://jcf.gov.jm/stats/*

100,000). As the evidence shows, some of the deadliest cities across the globe are in the Americas and violence is linked to high homicides, drug trafficking, organised crime, inter- and intra-gang wars, political instability, domestic and sexual disputes (Woody 2018).

Gangs traffic drugs and small arms through the porous national borders of the Caribbean region along three main routes: (1) Western Colombia to Central America and Mexico, (2) Mexico into the United States (US) and (3) Colombia to Jamaica to the Bahamas and into the US. The main transhipment points for cocaine, marijuana and small arms in the region are Puerto Rico, the Bahamas and Jamaica (Tulchin and Espach 2000).

The Caribbean is a crucial geographic corridor for the United States "war on drugs"; it is the 'transit zone' between South America and North America. Ivelaw Griffith (1997, 2004) and others, including S.H. Decker and M.T. Chapman (2008), maintain that the Caribbean is, "an important area for understanding drug smuggling because of its proximity to source and destination countries as well as its long history as a site for smuggling illegal goods and for piracy" (Decker and Chapman 2008, 55).

Along with its long history of illegal transhipment and piracy, the Caribbean has small and vulnerable economies that offer opportunities for drug smuggling. A 2008 study by the UNODC reported that despite successful interception measures, the Caribbean remains a significant corridor for drug trafficking and gun smuggling because of its historical, language, commercial and tourist ties to consumer countries to the North. Central and South America (especially criminal elements in Colombia and Mexico) are the dominant drug trafficking players across the Americas. The Caribbean corridor is important to the "producer state" (producers in countries that grow and manufacture illicit drugs such as marijuana and cocaine) traffickers. Drug dealers transhipped an estimated 10 tons of cocaine through Jamaica in 2005 and the United Nations Office on Drugs ranked the nation in the top six "source countries" for cannabis resin [marijuana] from 2004 to 2006 (UNODC 2008). The Dominican Republic, meanwhile, according to a 2008 UNOC Report, "is being used as a command, control and communications centre for drug operations in the Caribbean…It is a place to store drugs before its onward shipment to Puerto Rico and the United States".[8]

Drug trafficking through the Caribbean region connects Jamaica to a larger transnational political economy. Dons in Jamaica have engaged in drug trafficking and transhipment enterprises from as early as the 1980s. The drug trade between South and North America and Europe has allowed Jamaican dons to enrich themselves. Their involvement in narco-trafficking facilitated a shift from their near complete dependence on political parties for status and resources to a more self-reliant and autonomous standing. Dons changed from being 'political' in their orientations to being much more drug-focused (Campbell 2020; Blake 2013 and Sives 2002). Drug trafficking helped to enrich and empower dons through the money and guns they were able to acquire from dealing with producers, such as the Colombian drug cartels for whom they served as protectors of cocaine coming through Jamaican ports en route to North America and the UK.

The 2000s saw a new development as a "gun for drugs" trade emerged between Jamaica and Haiti. This exchange has increased the stockpile of guns available to criminal groups and gangs in the island. Chapter five provides evidence concerning the influence of drug and gun trafficking on the power of dons in Jamaican garrison neighbourhoods.

Governance and State Power

Governance refers to the process and act of ruling. It is not solely government-centred but instead also involves the actions of non-state entities such as non-governmental (NGOs), international non-governmental organisations (INGOs) and industries in delivering public goods and services (Kitthananan 2006; Pierre, 2000; Rhodes 2000; Rosenau 2000). Governance and governing also involve the input of perverse and criminal (or criminalised) players. Several scholars, especially those that study Latin America, include the influence of criminal actors on the processes of governance within and across the borders of the state (Arias 2006; Koonings and Kruijt 2007; Jones and Rodgers 2009). Other scholars, such as Diego Gambetta (1993), Philip Gounev and Vincenzo Ruggiero (2012) and Vadim Volkov (2002), have investigated how organised criminal groups have influenced the structure of politics and governance in Europe (especially in Italy and Eastern Europe). The literature on the Caribbean region minimally explores the impact that such criminal actors have on governance, especially at the local community level. *Don Dada* addresses that lacuna in the literature.

The state now exists in a globalised and transnational environment in which non-state actors are playing economic and political roles within its borders (Briquet 2010; Holston 2008; Strange 1996). These participants come from the private sector (market), civil society organisations and transnational governance bodies such as the International Monetary Fund (IMF) and the World Bank. In addition, non-state entities include influential local and transnational organised criminal networks that exert considerable political and economic pressure of their own (Blake 2013; Bowling 2010; Briquet 2010 and Schendel 2005). The state, in many developing nations, is becoming increasingly criminalised and "shadow versions" of it are being created via globalisation processes. For example, the drug trade, money laundering and offshore banking services have contributed to the criminalisation of the Belizean state (Duffy 2010).

The neoliberal turn in international politics created what some scholars refer to as "governance voids" in the developing world (Koonings and Kruijt 2007). The "hollowing out" of the Jamaican state became a consequence of the economic and political changes that accompanied neoliberal structural adjustment policies [SAPS]. Neoliberalism reduced the material leverage of the Jamaican government to provide its garrison constituents with satisfactory public services. It was not business as usual for the Jamaican political elite, and they began to lose the firm grip they had enjoyed over their garrison clients in the 1960s and 1970s. The governance literature (Chhotray and Stoker 2009; Stivers 2008; Matthews 1998) suggests that a "power shift" is taking place at the national and international levels, in which the state is losing its monopoly of control over its national borders. Pierre (2000) argues that state-centric analyses of power and authority within the nation-state are not as potent as they used to be. Economic globalisation has given rise to non-state actors from the market and civil society that now influence decision-making and governance at the international, national and sub-national levels.

Susan Strange (1996) has argued that globalisation has diffused state power among non-governmental actors. She posits that the state is retreating from its position of authority and control in the economy, public service delivery, and security. She has concluded that "criminal organisations have stepped in to fill states' regulatory and governance roles through marketised and informal systems of control" (see Strange in Arias 2006; 41). The 'legal–illegal nexus' spurred by the changes resulting from neoliberalism (Ruggiero 2002, 2012) highlights the interface between organised criminal actors and institutions of the economy and the state.

Ruggiero and others, including Volkov (2002) and Tilly (1985), contend that organised criminal groups/actors are social organisations that engage in multiple 'transactions' with various legitimate actors. These authors encourage analysts to view groups such as the Russian or the Italian Mafiosi as criminal networks that include several actors from both the legitimate and the illegal world. Ruggiero refers to them as "fuzzy criminal actors" (2002).

Across Latin America and the Caribbean, violent non-state actors threaten the authority of governments and the legitimacy of law enforcement. These perverse actors also disrupt the stability and peace in local communities. State control is hollowed out by gangs and other organised criminal syndicates in major cities in countries such as El Salvador, Brazil, and Jamaica (Samper 2016; Warmington-Granston and Blake 2020). These actors are in the business (literally) of establishing turf and spatial control for their drug-running and contraband enterprises. Some scholars argue that in parts of Latin America, gangs, such as the Maras in Guatemala, have gained economic and military-style powers by reaping the financial benefits from drug trafficking (Arias 2017 and Cruz 2016). Reflecting on the Nicaraguan case with the pandillas (criminal gangs) Rodgers (2009) concluded these actors, "constitute a form of sub-political social structuration in contemporary urban Nicaragua, rather than the source of chaotic disorder they are generally perceived to represent (2009, 41). The roles that dons perform in Jamaican garrisons mimic the "sub-political social structuration" Rodgers observed in Nicaragua.

The porous nature of the Caribbean[9] and the governance voids among governments in the region gave rise to criminal non-state activities and actors. It is not a coincidence that dons began to engage in cocaine trafficking in the 1980s around the time the Jamaican state began to experience what scholars refer to as neoliberal "shocks" (Klein 2007; Calvet and Broto 2015). Neoliberal governance opened the Jamaican state and society to a minimised welfare programme and greater exposure to free market capitalism. In turn, neoliberal shocks created governance voids, especially in local communities in the region. Jamaican garrisons were no exception. Dons then began to provide garrisons with services, including the security of property and human safety in the absence of action, or the inefficient response of the local police – the JCF. Jamaican dons, within the span of three-plus decades after its independence (1962), slowly attained embedded status.

Embedded Governance

Embeddedness refers to social relationships built on reciprocal cooperation and measured trust. I use the concept of embeddedness to describe and interpret the relationship between dons and the residents of Brown Villa. It explains the popular appeal some dons have among people living in garrisons. Originally posited by Karl Polanyi, the concept of embeddedness is used by sociologists, anthropologists, and political scientists seeking to analyse criminological phenomena. Simone Ghezzi and Enzo Mingione (2007) argue that it considers the conditions and contexts within which social action takes place: "embeddedness expresses the notion that social actors can be understood and interpreted only within relational, institutional and cultural contexts and cannot be seen as atomised decision-makers maximising their own utilities" (11).

James D. Montgomery (1998) posits that actors are not atomised individuals, but rather are locked into social networks that shape their actions. He reflects that "embeddedness typically involves long-term relationships characterised by mutual cooperation and trust in spite of the potential for opportunism … I trust you because I calculate that your short-run benefit from an opportunistic defection is outweighed by your long-run benefit from continued cooperation" (93).

Calculated trust, though in some measure perverse, is an important dimension of the embedded power base dons developed among garrison residents, elected officials and the police. Given the functions dons carry out in garrisons over time, most residents learn to invest their trust in these individuals who feed them, provide economic opportunities, and help to ensure their survival. They invest trust in the don who protects them from outsiders that threaten their community's collective security. Garrison residents endow their dons with "legitimate power" as a form of reward for helping them to address their basic needs. Nonetheless, some dons use "coercive power" to embed themselves in garrison spaces.

According to Ghezzi and Mingione, embedded modes of social behaviour and relationships are connected to specific spatial, historical, and cultural elements. This observation highlights the empirical as well as analytical value of an embedded analysis of the study of the roles played by Jamaican dons. Barry Chevannes (2002) has argued that these informal community leaders sometimes serve as role models and are cultural icons, particularly among inner-city youth. Dons personify the glamour and prestige associated with "ghetto" life.[10] He contended that in many ways, dons are folk heroes to some garrison residents. Dons, such as Christopher "Dudus" Coke and Donald "Zekes" Phipps, enjoyed strong cultural appeal and connections to the communities in which they played important governance roles.[11]

Dons are violent entrepreneurs who use the manpower, organisational capacity and the "firepower" of their criminal networks and gangs to exercise control. Violence is one strategy of control dons employ; they also possess economic prowess that gives them an embedded governing status inside Jamaica's garrison communities. *Don Dada* takes a second look at the perspectives on the state and governance; it makes room for the inclusion of perverse non-state actors in the discussion of legitimacy and power within and across pockets of the state and society.

Research Approach: Methods and Fieldwork

This is a single case study of one Jamaican garrison community, which has several smaller districts. The research site selected offered an opportunity to examine and describe the role(s) and functions that dons perform in garrison neighbourhoods. A qualitative research design was used to organise the sampling, data collection and analysis of the information gathered. This methodological approach facilitated a localised, contextually rich description and interpretation of the collected data on dons in a cluster of communities in the downtown Kingston area. For purposes of participant and researcher safety, the research site, place names and participants have been anonymised. Additionally, the pseudonym 'Brown Villa' is used to replace the real name of the research site.

A snow-balled sample size of 44 participants was interviewed during fieldwork research done in 2011 and 2012. Table 1.1 lists those interviewed by category. Follow-up fieldwork was conducted in 2019 where an additional 15 new participants were interviewed. Along with interviews, unobtrusive observation within Brown Villa and document analysis of Government of Jamaica national security policies and Jamaican newspaper articles formed the basis of the central data collection strategies employed.

Table 1.1: Interviewee List by Category

VT001-Journalist	VT002-NGO Director	VT025-NGO
VT003-Academic	VT004-NGO Director	VT026-Senior Police
VT005-Journalist	VT006-NGO	VT027-Former Gang Member
VT007-Clergy/CBO	VT008-Resident/CBO	VT028-NGO
VT009-Police	VT010-Clergy	VT029-Elected Official
VT011-Resident	VT012-NGO Director/ CBO	VT030-State Official
VT013-Social Worker		VT031-Police
VT015-Resident/CBO	VT014-Elected Official	VT032-Resident/CBO
VT017-Elected Official	VT016-NGO	VT033-NGO
VT019-Resident	VT018-Police	VT034-Ret. Police
VT021-Resident/CBO	VT020-Clergy/CBO	VT035-Resident/CBO
VT023-Senior Police	VT022-Senior Police	VT036-Police
	VT024-Clergy	VT037-Resident
		VT038- Senior Police
		VT039-Academic
		VT040-Former Gang Member
		VT041-Ret. Police
		VT042-Former Gang Member

NGO: Non-governmental organization
CBO: Community based organization

Book Structure

Chapter two, entitled "The Don's Power: Evolution, Typology, and Roles", unpacks who Jamaican dons are, their connection to the political history of the nation-state and how the macro-economic volatilities of the late 1970s into the 1980s transformed their power and the subsequent roles they perform. All dons are not the same. In this chapter, a taxonomical assessment is laid out that helps us to differentiate among, street, area and mega don types. This chapter explains the socio-political and cultural context within which Jamaican dons emerged and transformed over time. Having laid out a descriptive analysis of who dons are, in chapter three, "The Criminalisation of the Jamaica State", a theoretical framework explores the functions of the state and the impact local and transnational socio-economic and political patterns have on the nature of governance. As it turned out, organised crime, in the form of narcotic and weapons trading re-structured parts of the Jamaican state and society.

Chapter four, entitled "Brown Villa: The Jamaican Garrison Context", examines a cluster of communities in the downtown metro area of Kingston. These community districts are archetypes of the Jamaican garrison environment and lived experience. With an anaemic state presence and authority inside Brown Villa, residents experience several challenges associated with gang warfare, unemployment, poor housing and the degradation of public spaces and services (roads, drains, community health centres and police stations). Communities like Brown Villa are socially alienated and isolated from mainstream Jamaican society and residents feel a sense of socio-cultural marginalisation. Dons take advantage of the socio-cultural, economic, and political exclusion these communities experience and in turn, establish themselves as embedded despots.

In chapter five, entitled "Drugs and Dons: From Partisan Puppets to Ghetto Governors", the social power that dons have inside garrison communities and the specific roles they perform are explored in detail. This chapter takes note of the influence of globalisation and the neoliberal market forces that helped to liberalise licit and illicit commerce and trade. Drug and gun trafficking were game changers for Jamaican dons; it made them more powerful and independent of their earlier (1960s to 1970s) political partisan bosses. With the dawn of the twenty-first century, dons establish themselves as powerful forces to be reckoned with inside Jamaica's garrison spaces.

In contributing to the development of an institutional and social resolution to the problem of donmanship and the attendant violence and disorder that comes with it, chapter six, "Conclusion: Disempowering Jamaican Dons", reiterates the main findings and arguments presented in the book. This chapter describes the state-initiated policies to dismantle dons and gangs and provides an evaluation of their effectiveness. Suggestions of some pathways to dissolving the social, economic, and political power of Jamaica's dons are provided.

TWO

The Don's Power: Evolution, Typology, and Roles

Introduction

The Jamaican don is a non-state actor who wields considerable power and control in garrisons. These individuals contribute to the social instability that characterises these inner-city neighbourhoods as they are at the centre of organised crime, such as drug and gun trafficking, extortion rackets, robbery, international lottery frauds and even human trafficking.[1] In the Jamaican garrison context, dons/gangs often commit violent acts associated with political conflicts and turf warfare. Some also, however, perform social welfare and economic roles in their communities that afford them legitimacy and a measure of authority among residents. The problem that confronts the Jamaican state is that dons have enjoyed almost complete dominance in garrison communities across the Kingston Metropolitan Area (the parishes of Kingston, St Andrew, and St Catherine) from as early as the late 1960s.

Dons' dominance is reflected in the strong popular support they receive in garrisons, especially among youths. Dons, as one respondent said during an interview session, "decide who lives and who dies, they decide when the war starts and when it should end" (Interviewee: VT021).[2] Max Weber (1978) has defined power as "the chance of a man or a number of men to realise their own will even against the resistance of others who are participating in the action" (926). Power then implies one's or a group's capacity to exercise control and domination over another. One has power when he has the capacity to get another person to act in a particular way; this ability is supported using sanctions – whether negative or positive. In some cases, a person may have legitimate grounds upon which to exercise power; the state using law enforcement, for example, has the 'right' to undertake that responsibility.

Hindess (1996) has grappled with the concept of power and suggested that it involves both the capacity and the right to exercise control. Power involves both elements of coercion and consent. In this regard, Hindess concludes, "social power, then, is a matter of domination on the one hand and collective organisation on the other" (7). Jamaican dons are embedded governing figures that have acquired power and a measure of authority in their communities over time. They have been, in some cases, entrusted with power with the active consent of garrison residents.

Bertram H. Raven and John R. R. French, Jr (1958) developed a five-point basis for evaluating "social power" several decades ago: reward power, coercive power, legitimate power, referent power and expert power. Their analysis of coercive and legitimate power applies to the analysis of dons and garrisons in Jamaica. In their view, coercive power results from one person's ability to sanction another negatively for non-compliance with their orders or wish (wishes). They contend legitimate power emerges when a person or group is believed to have the right to exercise control over another. The use of force by those who possess legitimate power is appropriate and, in some cases, necessary (for example, by the police to protect the public).

Dons have power in garrison communities; they sometimes use violence or its threat to compel residents to comply with their orders and respect their status. Over time, some dons have managed to build a relationship with the residents of "their" garrisons based on reciprocal trust; they provide welfare benefits to neighbourhood inhabitants and, in return, those residents accord dons legitimacy and authority. William Gorgan (2012) argues that the case of Christopher "Dudus" Coke neatly reflects the social power of Jamaican dons. He contends that "years of Coke's patronage to the community had given the don an intensely loyal following among some of Tivoli's residents, at the same time creating an atmosphere of dependency on the gangster which permeated the garrison" (Gleaner 2012).[3]

Historical Context: Politics, Economy, and Dons

Carlene J. Edie (1991) argues that to understand the deeply interconnected relationship among Jamaica's elite classes, political parties, and urban inner-city communities, we must first understand the nation's colonial and post-colonial political history. British colonialism in the Caribbean had the effect of producing political systems based on patronage, a polarised partisan political culture, and the monopolisation of power by economic and political elites. Edie maintains that a patron-client relationship characterised politics in the decolonisation and post-independence [after 1962] periods in Jamaica.

In "From Manley to Seaga: The Persistence of Clientelist Politics in Jamaica", Edie argued that political violence in Jamaica resulted from a patronage system in which both patrons and clients made material and non-material exchanges. Officials of either major political party, the Peoples National Party-PNP or the Jamaica Labour Party-JLP, served as patrons, and they received political support and assent from their community clients who in turn gained access to state largesse and political "pork". With citizens receiving benefits from the patron, they engaged in violent confrontations with rival and opposing groups to maintain access to those resources. "JLP or PNP" membership entailed social connotations and forged communal identities. One's political affiliation could not be detached from the community in which one resided or from one's trade union affiliation; they were inseparable (Edie 1991).

Partisan politics became a part of the identity of many Jamaicans, especially those who resided in garrisons, and the identifications those ties forged helped to foster the development of political tribalism. Anthony Payne (1995) has argued that by 1980, groups participated in violent confrontations in which "both political parties organised their own-armed gangs as the means to defend their supporters' access to state patronage" (2). As this argument suggests, dons in Jamaica have played the roles of political enforcer and area leader for one of the two major political parties (PNP or JLP) in garrison neighbourhoods.

During the 1960s and 1970s, dons functioned in these central roles on behalf of their party bosses. For their efforts, these individuals received public contracts and spoils; that is, the reward of government contracts for the dons' support of party bosses. They also received protection from police investigations and arrest as political party leaders ensured their compensation for services rendered. However, a change took place in 1980 as the two main parties in Jamaica reacted to global economic changes.

The economic ideology of neoliberalism[4] and the resulting structural adjustment policies of the International Monetary Fund, for example, meant that the Jamaican state had to scale back on its social welfare programmes. Since the late 1970s (1978–80), successive governments in Jamaica, as elsewhere in the Americas, have curtailed or otherwise sought to minimise their footprint in governing the country (Harvey 2005). Consequently, the two major political parties have enjoyed a much-diminished stock of patronage to extend to their surrogates and enforcers.

In response, by the early 1980s, dons began to engage in a range of other legitimate and illegitimate activities that enabled them to reduce their dependence on their traditional partisan bosses. With their involvement in the drug trade between South America and North America/UK, for example, dons became wealthier and had access to more guns and arms. The money and weapons they acquired from drug trafficking allowed some of them to play social welfare and community security roles; they now had the capacity to arm their neighbourhood turfs with hired militia and supply them with handguns and high-powered weapons.[5] The emergence of these new roles facilitated the dons' increasing standing in garrison communities. Some of these informal community leaders filled the vacuum left by the retreating neoliberal Jamaican state and began to play roles and perform functions the state was either unwilling or unable to perform. Rattary (2001) has commented on the socio-economic embeddedness[6] of these non-state actors in their "home" garrisons by arguing that dons, "are the by-products of our country's socio-economic and bio-political transgressions. The dons have flourished because the inner-city people have chosen to symbolically co-exist with them as a means of survival" (*Gleaner* December 11, 2001).[7]

Dons became the new hegemonic figures in garrisons during the 1980s and that trend continued in succeeding decades. The 'neoliberal turn' in governmental policies and governance across the Americas in the 1980s and 1990s and the simultaneous rise of the Colombian cocaine trade, fostered this turn of events. Hume N. Johnson and Joseph L. Soeters (2008) have observed that the "radical shifts in the global economy after 1980 had the effect of further shifting the power dynamics in Jamaica's slum dwellings". Neoliberal shifts, they have argued, made "way for the consolidation of a notorious dynasty of dons and the retreat of civil leadership" in Jamaica's garrisons (173). Marlyn J. Jones (2002) and Amanda Sives (2002) have also reported an increase in drug-related gang and gun violence in the same period.

Dons emerged out of the politically polarised periods of national independence in Jamaica and the proxy ideological and political conflicts of the Cold War. Scholarship and interviewee responses indicate that dons are creatures of Jamaica's polarised partisan history. They tend to dominate garrison communities that suffer from poor infrastructure development, limited social services and inadequate delivery of public goods, such as sanitation and roads (Campbell 2020; Leslie 2010). In several garrisons, dons have filled a vacuum left by the state. In Brown Villa, for example, residents interviewed pointed out that when they want recourse to justice for criminal acts, such as rape or robbery, they are more willing to turn to dons than to the police. Regarding employment opportunities, residents contend that they often receive jobs from dons to work as task labourers on construction sites, or to be workers within a dons' transportation network (public and private taxi/ bus services), and/or their grocery and retail clothing businesses.

In May 2010, the Jamaican state started making a concerted attempt to re-establish its control over garrisons.[8] The operation to extradite Christopher "Dudus" Coke spurred an island-wide joint military and police campaign to uproot gangs and dons in garrison neighbourhoods. The national initiative led to a decline in Jamaica's homicide and violent crime rates. However, the incursion into Tivoli Gardens resulted in the death of seventy-three persons and the recovery of only four weapons. Scores of residents and several local human rights groups, including Jamaicans for Justice (JFJ), decried what they considered the inhumane tactics of the police and military units. According to the JFJ, the national government's respect for human rights has plummeted since the May 2010 incursion. In 2010 alone, the police and military accounted for one-fifth of Jamaica's violent deaths (Gomes April 7, 2011).[9]

Since the extradition of Dudus, the security landscape in Jamaica has been unpredictable and volatile. While there have been periods of calm where law enforcement managed to reassert its position of authority, violence related to dons and gangs remains a serious problem in Jamaica. The island's current National Security Minister Dr Horace Chang notes that in 2020, 75 per cent of all gangs in Jamaica are established in the Kingston Central, Kingston East, and Kingston West divisions. According to data from the Ministry of National Security, these gangs which are led by various types of dons, are responsible for most of the homicides in the Kingston metro area (*Jamaica Observer* 23 October 2020). In March 2020, according to data from *Statistica*, Jamaica recorded a homicide rate of approximately 47.4 homicides per 100,000 inhabitants in the country in 2019. This figure is an increase in the 2018 homicide rate which was 47 per 100,000 inhabitants. To put this into regional context, in 2019, Venezuela was the only country that ranked above Jamaica for homicides with a rate of 60.3. and Honduras was third with a rate of 41.2 per 100,000 inhabitants.[10] Violence is one feature of the social power that Jamaican dons possess. It is also used as a tool to acquire and maintain a status of control and order.

Don Typological Pyramid

The typology of Jamaican dons below distinguishes among *mega dons, area dons* and *street dons*. This taxonomy is important since it is imperative to be clear that not all garrisons have the same kinds of dons. The category of "don" is not homogeneous, and an appropriate identification requires a contextual analysis.

A *mega don* can perform a wide range of roles in his garrison because of his access to large sums of money, resources, personnel, and an arsenal of weapons. Many residents view this kind of don as a saviour to fatherless boys, single mothers and young men and women who find it difficult to gain employment. The mega don has strong partisan connections, is very rich and operates multiple businesses, both legitimate and illegitimate. These individuals receive political contracts from the state to repair roads, build bridges and construct homes.[11] His power transcends any single garrison, and he enjoys strong network connections with law enforcement officials (especially the police) and the business community, and he usually has transnational associations as well. Internationally, the mega don can access overseas markets for drugs and gun trafficking. These individuals exercise geographical jurisdiction in more than one garrison community; Christopher Coke, for example, controlled several satellite communities in addition to his garrison "headquarters", Tivoli Gardens.

The *area don*, meanwhile, also has strong partisan ties and considerable wealth, usually gained from drug trafficking and legitimate sources, including government contracts. The principal difference between the mega and the area don is that the latter tends to control a specific community or territory. The area don does not have the strong transnational links and resource base (money and guns) that the mega don can access and activate. The data gathered for this research suggest that some area and street dons report to mega dons. That is, some area dons have network associations and partnerships with mega dons. In Brown Villa, interviewees pointed out that one don in their community (I classify him as an area don) had business connections with a mega don from an adjoining community. The relationships among different types of dons are explored in chapters four and five. Area dons often have dominance over one geographic location.

Finally, the *street don* is, as the name suggests, a lower-level community leader. These individuals control a street or streets in a garrison community. Brown Villa had street dons who played minimal welfare roles in their communities in comparison to the community's past and current area dons. Mega dons differ primarily from area dons in their ability to exercise cross-community power. The street don, meanwhile, has limited funds and very few guns at his disposal. One interview respondent observed, "gun-sharing" and "renting" is prominent among street gangs and dons (Interviewee: VT006). These gang leaders have partisan connections, but their interaction with political actors such as Members of Parliament is episodic and intensifies as elections draw near. Street dons have associations with, and in most cases are appointed by, more senior area or mega dons to control specific turf. These territories (turf) can be of economic significance, such as bus parks and business districts. They can also have political importance, as dons still provide services to partisan actors in exchange for government contracts and minimal surveillance from law enforcement officials (police). This typology represents a conceptual and empirical addition to the literature on garrisons and dons in Jamaica.

Alexandra Colak and Jenny Pearce (2009) in their examination of communities in Brazil and Guatemala have labelled inner-city neighbourhoods that reflect similar patterns of violence and poverty to that evidenced in Jamaica's garrisons, "parallel communities" (4–6). They argue that such communities can emerge where there is a strong state (Brazil) or a weak one (Guatemala). The key characteristic of these areas is that residents do not rely on the state for their security or protection. They contend:

> In these communities, the state is normally not capable of providing basic services, including security, and its intervention is often intermittent, reactive, and disciplinary rather than protective. One of the characteristics of these parallel communities is that state institutions such as the police are not the main, or best equipped, or even desirable providers of protection. Alternative actors normally connect to lucrative illegal or informal economic activities, and to facilitate these, they replace the state and often act interchangeably as coercive 'protectors' for some sectors of the population creating protection rackets.[12] (5)

The Jamaican case, based on the findings in Brown Villa, reveals that dons play similar roles of protection and security in their garrison neighbourhoods. Garrisons are shadow versions of the state rather than parallel communities as Colak and Pearce contend. Garrisons are mini-states within the larger Jamaican state where dons are entrusted with the powers of dispute resolution, the maintenance of law, order, and security (perverse albeit), and the capacity to administer localised systems of welfare distribution.

Roles

Roles refer to the social, political, and economic functions carried out by individuals, groups or organisations. Scholars note that roles are contingent upon social situations and that they are in many ways socially constructed. Historical forces shape roles and they evolve over time (Montgomery 1994; 1998). Dons in Jamaica derive their legitimacy, popularity, and power from their capacities to deliver material and immaterial 'goods' to garrison residents. According to John Rapley (2003), dons' roles and functions are shaped in part by a necessity to please community inhabitants. He believes that the power of the garrison don must be "set against the fact that his constituents demand much for their loyalty…more than anyone, the don fears his own people" (27). The fieldwork findings support this view in part as some dons, especially the mega and area dons, are highly invested in securing their legitimacy and popularity among residents as a means of ensuring their longevity.

The current literature on 'Jamaican dons' per se is limited; there is more work on the socio-economic and political characteristics of garrisons (Edmonds 2016; Figueroa 1992; Harriott 2008; Harriott 2004; Sives 2002; Stone 1973, 1980). Previous studies reference dons as a part of their larger garrison environment. While I provide a contextual analysis of garrison communities is provided, the central focus is the evolution of the roles of dons and the impact of their donmanship on residents in the spaces they live and operate.[13]Electoral mobilisation and political intimidation (two functions traditionally undertaken by dons) are comprehensively examined in the Jamaican-don-garrison literature (Edie 1991; Sives 1998, 2002, 2010; Stone 1986). However, other roles this enquiry found to be significant for some dons, including the provision of security and protection; social welfare and dispute resolution, have received much less attention in existing scholarship. Some earlier works (Blake 2013; Munroe and Blake 2017; Warmington-Granston and Blake 2020) on the topic have addressed this gap in the literature.

There is a non-violent dimension to donmanship in Jamaica. Undoubtedly, dons are directly connected with violence (shootings and murder); however, as laid out in chapter five, they also provide social welfare and public order services in garrison environments. Only a small list of other scholars (such as Jaffe 2019; Campbell 2020) have looked at some of the non-violent actions of Jamaican dons. *Don Dada* identifies four central roles (violent and non-violent) that dons carry out in the garrison community of Brown Villa. These include: (1) Community

Welfare; (2) Security and Protection; (3) Partisan Mobilisation; and (4) Law, Order and Conflict Resolution via Jungle Justice measures.

At the research design stage, it was assumed that dons perform all the above-listed roles inside garrisons. As the field research progressed, it was discovered that only some dons performed those roles. The extent and nature of their involvement in these activities were discovered through the data collection and analysis process. The law, order, and conflict resolution role has enabled dons of all types to use force and fear as a means of embedding themselves in community governance. Not all types of dons perform all four roles. The street don, for example, rarely performs welfare roles in his community, unlike his area or mega don counterparts.

Jamaican dons operate as de facto governors of garrisons and these communities are shadow versions of the larger official Jamaican state (Blake 2013). Garrison residents often depend on dons and their organised criminal syndicates to provide security for their communities, and as I will show later in the book, access to a localised version of justice and social order. This power of social control and authority is accorded to dons in garrisons given the realities of an overburdened and unequal judicial system. There is a perception among garrison residents that the state's official law enforcement and court systems seldom guarantee justice. In interviews with residents of Brown Villa, they contend that don-ordered justice in garrisons is swift and direct, and it prevents individuals or groups from disrupting the social order and stability of the community.

The weakening of the Jamaican state, coupled with the rise of alternate sources of illegal revenue that globalisation offered, facilitated the embedding of the rule of dons. James D. Montgomery (1998) contends that embedded people are not atomised individuals but are instead members of social networks that shape their actions. Based on the roles dons carry out in garrisons, residents have learned over time to invest their trust in them. Community members view these individuals as helping to feed them, provide economic opportunities and protect them from outsiders whom they consider threats.

THREE

The Criminalisation of the State

Introduction

Dons are governance figures embedded in garrisons. Previous studies have approached the issue of the power of Jamaican dons by contending that these roles arose from political leader – client relationships during the late 1960s and early 1970s (Edie 1991, 1994; Sives 1998; Stone 1986). Nonetheless, in my view, clientelism does not fully capture the temporal shifts in the relationship that dons have had with the state and with garrison residents in the post-1970s period. While not denying the role of clientelism, I seek to describe the dynamics of this phenomenon more completely by employing governance theories and the concept of embeddedness. I add to traditional governance frames the concept of embeddedness to describe and interpret how dons have managed to retain their spheres (economic, political, and social) of power and control inside garrison communities, despite attempts by law enforcement agencies to remove them.

Anthony Harriott (2008) has suggested the Caribbean region has a sub-culture of violence that manifests itself in its high homicide rates, strong gang cultures and prevalence of organised crime. Dons long have used violence to instil fear among residents as a tool for sustaining their power in garrisons (Blake 2013; Clarke 2006; Rapley 2003). Unbridled force and local versions of extreme justice (called jungle justice by garrison residents) are examples of coercive power that dons employ to intimidate residents and ensure their support (Levy 2009). Chapter one mentioned the works of Raven and French (1958) and Hindess (1996) on power. "Coercive power" and "reward power" were singled out as appropriate ways of viewing the legitimacy, control, and authority that dons tend to amass and exercise in Jamaica's garrisons. Gareth Jones and Dennis Rodgers (2009) and Caroline Moser and Cathy McIlwaine (2001) have argued that in some Latin American countries, gangs, such as the Maras in Guatemala and the Pandilleros in Nicaragua, have gained economic and military-style powers by engaging in drug trafficking activities. Like Jamaica's dons and their associated gangs, the Maras and Pandilleros exercise considerable influence on the urban inner-city communities in which their leaders and members reside.

Several scholars (Chevannes 1992; Edie 1991; Figueroa 1992; Stone 1985, 1986) have comprehensively addressed the political and socio-economic evolution of garrison communities in Jamaica. However, to date, only a handful of researchers have systematically studied how dons emerged and how their roles have evolved over time. Accordingly, this chapter explores the literature that examines the historical development of garrison communities in Jamaica with an eye to what it may suggest specifically concerning the evolution of dons. The history behind Jamaican dons begins with the political context (1960s into 1970s) of a deeply polarised and confrontational partisan democratic system (Edie 1991).

A review of the scholarship on the garrison don contextualises the rise of these leaders and the important temporal points and processes that facilitated significant changes in their social power and the different roles they perform over time. Dons' roles have shifted from functions locked in a top-down dyadic relationship with partisan officials to becoming embedded powerful actors that have a variety of relationships with garrison residents. As their power base expanded, dons and partisan actors increasingly came to act more as equals in their relationships. This change, which occurred in the 1980s, signalled that dons were no longer simply taking orders from elected officials (Sives 2002). Instead, the relationship of these local figures with governmental and party leaders shifted in practice from a uni-directional form to a bi-directional one. John Rapley (2003) has suggested that the "tail is now wagging the dog" as dons have become autonomous powerful figures to whom partisan actors now often defer. In some cases, dons, and the gangs they lead, literally have gained territorial control over garrisons from the official arms of the state (police and elected representatives).

According to Rapley:

> The dons, in short, have carved out small fiefdoms for themselves where they can operate pretty much with impunity. ... The problem for the police is not that law and order have broken down in garrisons, quite the contrary. It is that they (police) are trying to reclaim a role for their law and to restore or preserve what they can of their relevance. (28)

In Rapley's view, the Jamaican state lost its capacity to "impose its sovereignty" in garrisons and had to "negotiate" such standing. Given this circumstance, the police often found themselves bargaining with dons to reassert the lost authority of the state (28–29).

Additionally, previous scholarship on the political history of Jamaica suggests strongly that the nation's civic history has long been tied to polarised partisan identities and political violence. These have contributed to the creation of the urban spaces now called garrisons (Gunst 1995; Lacey 1977; Levy 1996). The don emerged in these communities, and their titles/roles evolved from being "rude bwoys" in the 1960s to "area leaders" during the 1970s and 1980s. By the 1980s, the term don described men who had significant but informal leadership roles inside the inner-city neighbourhoods of the Kingston Metropolitan Area. Beyond their community leadership status, dons have long also been associated with garrison violence, gang culture, organised criminality, and the inculcation of fear among residents (Headly 1994; Harriott 2002, 2004, 2008). The concept of embedded governance actors provides theoretical support to the proposition that dons are not merely pawns within patron-client networks. Instead, they have evolved into governing players themselves, who often operate outside the realm of patron-client associations and relationships alone.

The capacity of the state is closely associated with the literature on governance (Tilly 2007), democracy, power, neoliberalism, violence, and organised crime (drug and gun trafficking in particular). These topics are important to the concerns and objectives of this research; therefore, they form an important part of the literature reviewed. Studies on the state inform our collective understanding of the functions it performs and the constraints it faces in providing education, health care and security. Perspectives on power and democracy are important to the aims of this book too as they help to explain the sphere of control and authority that individuals and groups have within the borders of the state. Providing security to residents in garrison communities, granting them access to welfare support by sending children to school and giving cash allotments to household heads are functions built on democratic principles of governance (Dahl 1999; Diamond and Morlino 2005).

Violence and organised crime must be central concerns to understanding dons and garrisons. The literature on violence, particularly in Latin America and the Caribbean, helps to contextualise the 'roots' of gang warfare and organised criminality such as extortion, drug and gun trafficking. These different pieces of literature are used to present the case that Jamaican dons, as have other non-state criminal actors elsewhere in the world (for example, the Italian Mafia) become involved in local and international illegal activities as a means of prolonging their tenure as community power brokers. The governance literature suggests that in situations such as that in Jamaica characterised by a failing, weak or absent state, other actors outside its official structures will emerge and perform its functions (Arias 2006, 2017; Tilly 2007). A similar phenomenon has occurred in other countries in Latin America and the Caribbean in which the retreat of the state has given rise to criminal non-state actors assuming governance or governance-like roles inside local communities. These include Nicaragua, Guatemala, and Mexico (Briquet 2010; Jones and Rogers 2009). In settings where social, economic, and political forms of exclusion preclude the realisation of desirable societal goals such as security, employment and proper housing via legitimate means, criminal networks and activities become viable paths to social mobility and inclusion (Harrell and Peterson 1992; Young 1999).

The State

By investigating the influence of informal community leaders such as Jamaica's dons, a critique of the state and its capacity to govern in the era of neoliberal globalisation naturally arises. But what is the state, and what functions is it expected to perform? Max Weber (1970) has defined the state as a social community in which force and violence are legitimated in the relationship between governments and their citizens. It is a "human community that claims the monopoly of legitimate use of force" (Weber 1970, 78). Liberal scholars, including Robert Nozick (1974), have argued that the state's main function is to provide security and protect the individual rights of its citizens to exercise their liberty. Nozick argues for a minimal state. The state from this perspective has the main prerogative to ensure the safety of its citizens from external attacks and the responsibility of refereeing and settling internal conflicts. The state also is responsible for creating an environment that promotes the economic rights and opportunities of those it governs. How best to do this is where Nozick and other theorists part company. Yoram Barzel (2002) concludes that the creation of market space and networks of roads are crucial ways in which the state can promote the economic livelihood of individuals. In his view, "designating a central space to serve as a market is likely to further promote trade. What characterises a market is the free access to it and the common-property nature of its space" (189).

Elite theorists of the state (including Domhoff 1967; Michels 1959; Pareto 1976) have argued that only the interests of small powerful elite groups and individuals are responded to by the state. They go further to argue that these control the state. In their view, the state and its agencies are governed by a few. Marx (1967) and others (Miliband 1983; Poulantzas 1978) go a step further in arguing that the state is essentially the "executive committee of the bourgeoisie" and that power resides in the hands of the ruling elite class. The state, when viewed from this perspective, is a form of elite class social control and hegemony executed through the institutions of government (for example law enforcement). Erika Cudworth, Timothy Hall, and John McGovern have suggested meanwhile that the state is "self-regulating, serving to constrain and limit human action externally just as market laws constrain and limit economic agents" (110).

Garrison residents often perceive the Jamaican state, especially its judicial (courts) and law enforcement (police) institutions, as oppressive and predatory (Gray 2004). In terms of economic opportunities and social welfare, growing levels of inequality and poverty have alienated and isolated the blue-collar working and so-called lumpenproletariat classes in Jamaica. The neoliberal era, starting in the late 1970s, weakened the Jamaican state and thereby increased poverty and social inequality. This created a socio-economic environment and political space into which dons could emerge as serious governing actors.

Governance

Governance is essentially about ruling. Persons or institutions shape public policies and help to provide essential services such as health care, security, education, and housing. Miles Khaler and David A. Lake (2004) have defined governance as "that subset of restraints that rests on authority" (409). For them, governance involves the exercise of authority in which decisions are made by one actor and other actors are "expected to obey" (409). Kitthananan (2006), meanwhile, has argued that governance is about "governing", where the state plays a steering and partnering role in the processes of "improving public sector capacity" in the economy and society (2). Other writers (Pierre 2000; Rhodes 2000) have suggested that governance points to the capacity to get things done without relying on the power of government or its centralised authority alone. Rosenau (2000) has posited that governance refers to a system of ruling, which can encompass a wide range of agencies and institutions, including NGOs, non-profit groups and INGOs such as the Red Cross, public and private for-profit institutions, and other players (Pierre 2000, 171).

Scholars, including Oran Young (1999) and D. Roderick Kiewiet and Mathew D. McCubbins (1991), have argued that the capacity to exercise authority is an important feature of governance. They recognise that governance can occur at multiple scales and sights – transnational, international, national, sub-national and local. With globalisation, especially its neoliberal phase, sites of political authority have transitioned and migrated from the realm of the state alone. Other actors now share in the "delegation of authority" within the borders of the nation-state (Kiewiet and McCubbins 1991, 20). The literature is clear in contending that governance is not confined to government and its authority, but rather is about how power and public decision-making are shared among different state and non-state entities.

Governance perspectives are important to this study as they provide a tool for analysing political institutions as well as the national and global linkages among state and non-state actors. Pierre and Peters (2020) have argued that theories of governance should focus on the state; that is, on how the shift from "government" to "governance" has influenced the functions the state performs. They contend the state is a central player in society. Several scholars (Clarke 2006; Chevannes 1992; Gray 1994; Henry-Lee 2005; Johnson 2005; Levy 2009; Sives 2002; Stone 1985; Witter 1992) have suggested that the Jamaican state failed to maintain itself as an active player in society in the decades after its independence (1960s onwards), especially in providing public services to its urban inner-city communities.

The state in most developing countries suffers from what Tilly (2007) has termed "low capacity". He has contended that where there is a weak economy and poor bureaucratic structures for public service delivery (in areas such as transportation, health care, and security) the state's ability to govern is handicapped. He contends that where the state has a low capacity to govern, "democratisation" processes are negatively affected. For Tilly, democratisation is a process oriented in time and space, in which a state, depending on its capacity (whether "high" or "low"), can move toward or away from that state: "A regime is democratic to the degree that political relations between the state and its citizens feature broad equal, protected and mutually binding consultation" (13–14). A low-capacity democratic regime in Tilly's analysis is one in which the rights extended do not cover a wide "breadth" of citizens and "public politics" is exclusionary in character (14). In such nations, inequality among citizens is rife and there is minimal protection from the arbitrary use of force by the state (especially by the police and military). Tilly cited Jamaica as an example of a low-capacity democratic state. The limited capability of the Jamaican state to govern garrison spaces effectively, especially by the 1980s, allowed dons to garner socio-political power and embed themselves in these communities. During this period (1980s and 1990s), dons began to accept responsibility for some of the functions that the state was either unwilling or unable to perform.

Khaler and Lake (2004) and their colleagues have employed the concept of authority in a politically legitimising sense. Governance is employed similarly here. However, the concept of power is used to describe the capacity dons exercise in Jamaica's garrisons. Power, while it may include the application of authority and control, sometimes occurs without the political legitimacy with which it is often joined and that often is presupposed for states. Criminal non-state actors, such as Jamaica's dons or members of the Russian Mafia, do not possess legitimate political authority. Nonetheless, they are powerful actors who use force and material rewards to gain authoritative standing (perversely, some may argue) and control.

Criminalised Governance

The governance literature on the Caribbean region pays limited attention to criminal non-state actors as important brokers of power within and across the borders of the nation-state. Khaler and Lake (2004), in their analysis of the effects of globalisation on governance, focused on roles played by state and intergovernmental institutions; they did not consider the impact of non-state individuals and groups. They suggested that globalisation has had the effect of migrating authority upwards, from the state to the international level among global economic and political institutions such as the International Monetary Fund, the World Bank and the European Court of Justice. Globalisation and the neoliberal policies of a minimal state have had a similar effect on Jamaica's garrisons of migrating authority downwards to non-state criminal actors. The case examined here explores one example of the characteristics and impact of this downward migration of authority to illegal actors (in this case Jamaican dons). While it is not examined here, relevant scholarship suggests that the phenomenon probed in Jamaica has also obtained in other Caribbean and Latin American nations (Arias 2006; Baird 2012; Rodgers 2009).

Susan Strange (1996) and Enrique Desmond Arias (2006) have offered governance conceptualisations that include criminal and perverse actors. Arias (2006) has suggested that criminals must be fitted into the "political picture" when analysts examine governance structures in developing countries. To this end, he argues, "in developing countries, violent non-state actors operating through networks with civic and state actors play increasingly important roles in the control of space, people and resources" (10). This point is particularly significant here. Jamaican dons are important players in the organisation and control of garrison spaces. Indeed, as shown in the section on historical context, dons were central players in the exercise of political authority by the Jamaican state in garrison areas even before they acquired independent sources of funding and armoury. Dons assumed responsibility for controlling and distributing state largesse to politically loyal residents in garrisons beginning in the late 1960s (Edie 1984; Figueroa 1992).

In *Organised Crime and States: The Hidden Face of Politics*, Jean-Louis Briquet and Gilles Favarel-Garrigues (2010) advance the thesis that a "criminalisation of the state" is taking place in certain nations all over the globe. This perverse process accompanies the international flow of business, ideas, and capital. Crime, according to these authors, is becoming more transnational in character and interwoven with the administrative structures of the state in some developing nations. Favarel-Garrigues (2010), has pointed to the interconnectedness between the Mafia and politicians in Russia. He observed that "relations between politics and the Mafia derive their meaning less from parasitism than from commensalism, a term that acknowledges the state of symbiosis uniting two partners in a lasting association that presents no underlying threat to either party" (154–155). In the Jamaican context, Arias (2006) has argued that such a connection exists between elements of the criminal underworld in Kingston and certain political leaders and state actors (182). For her part, Rosaleen Duffy (2010) has suggested that "developing states have not been marginalised or left behind by globalisation, rather they are inextricably linked to the global system, often through transnational illicit trading networks, [that] become deeply embedded within the formal state apparatus and the legal trading system" (98).

Diego Gambetta's (1993) analysis of the Sicilian Mafia offers a provocative perspective on the ties of illegal/criminal actors to the state's formal economy. He contended that the Mafia provides a particular service, that of "protection" in the market space of the Sicilian economy. In his view, both legitimate and illegitimate actors seek to provide protection, which is essential for industry and commerce to flourish. Gambetta describes the Mafia as a "specific economic enterprise/

industry" in which the protection they provide represents an essential catalyst of economic exchange (1–5). Gambetta's work is important to studies of governance as it pushes interested analysts to re-think the nexus between what is legal and what is illegal. The Sicilian Mafia emerged and became embedded actors inside the state during the nineteenth century because of a persistent lack of trust in official government agencies to offer needed services to local businesspersons and landowners.

Vadim Volkov (2002) has referred to criminal non-state actors, such as the Russian Mafia, as "violent entrepreneurs" who use organisational methods that allow force/violence to be transformed into valuable commodities, including money (27). He argues further that "the concept of violent entrepreneurship is applicable not only to certain outlaw groups but also to legitimate agencies and even the state" (27). Volkov concluded that as private business multiplied and transactions in the marketplace increased, the need for partnerships between legitimate and illegal actors also rose.

Vincenzo Ruggiero (2012), summing up the influence that non-state criminal actors have in Italy on the state and the process of governance, has argued:

> Organised crime enjoys strong links with civil society… It can offer occupational opportunities to professional criminals on the one hand, and a variety of goods and services to purchasers, on the other. It may be highly integrated in the institutional arena, where it can forge partnerships with economic and political actors. (11–12)

Ruggiero's comments echoes the discussion on the strong links forged between elected officials of the PNP and the JLP and garrison dons.

In the developing world, neoliberal globalisation paved the way for non-state institutions and other players to emerge and eventually influence governance processes. Dons exercise governance at the local level in Jamaica. As David Held (2000) has noted in today's globalised international politics, "the locus of effective power can no longer be assumed to be national governments – effective power is shared, bartered, and struggled over by diverse forces and agencies at national, regional and international levels" (52).

Neoliberalism and Governance

Neoliberalism continues to reshape and transform the political economies of the globe, with far-reaching effects on the societies it has touched. David Harvey (2005) has described neoliberalism as a:

> Theory of political and economic practices that proposes that human well-being can best be advanced by liberating individual entrepreneurial freedoms. It embraces the harnessing of entrepreneurial freedom and skills within the broader institutional rubric of strong private property rights, free markets, and free trade. (2–3)

He notes further that within this institutional framework, the state has a minimalist and specialised role to play in providing security for private property (via police, military, and legal structures) and promoting the full and free functioning of the market. Rick Rowden (2009) has summarised the principal impacts of neoliberal claims since the 1980s for global health by contending that neoliberalism has had "deadly" effects on public health and the fight against HIV/AIDS, especially in the developing world, as such policies reduced public expenditure on health challenges and thereby often hobbled HIV treatment and prevention efforts. This peculiar form of development economics has led to an incremental withering away of health policies, which supported budgets that helped doctors, nurses and other health care workers address several critical infectious diseases (1–5).

Similarly, neoliberalism has had the "deadly" and perverse consequence of weakening state capacity in other sectors besides health in many developing countries. Neoliberal policies in Latin America and the Caribbean have undermined the capabilities of states located in those regions to provide education, job opportunities and human welfare services to their residents (Klak 1996, 1999). Data provided by the United Nations Development Programme in its Caribbean Human Development Report, 2012 indicate that the level of human development in the region has been undesirably low. During the period of the late 1970s into the 1980s, the adoption of neoliberal policies in Jamaica caused the government to cut back on state-sponsored welfare and social programmes. State funding for human development initiatives in the areas of literacy and skills training was hard hit by the neoliberal market-driven approach. In the Jamaican case, as with other countries in the Latin American and Caribbean (LAC) region, the situation worsened because of an escalating debt owed to international lending agencies such as the International Monetary Fund and the World Bank. National budgets in the LAC region were overwhelmed with servicing international debt and that meant that several social and economic programmes geared towards poverty reduction were side-tracked (Harris 2005). The UNDP report argued that violence and high homicide rates in the region are associated with its low levels of human development; the absence of legitimate and strong institutions as well as a dearth of inclusive systems of governing (8). Caribbean national leaders, at the time of independence (1960s in the English Caribbean), inherited states with weak capacities and social institutions that did not make alleviation of the suffering of the poor a priority. The neoliberal policies of structural adjustment (1980s–1990s) these states adopted did not strengthen the affected nations' social institutions nor did they improve the various states' capacities to provide public goods (income opportunities, education, health care, and housing) to their populations, poor and non-poor alike (UNDP 2012).

The political and economic changes wrought by neoliberalism provided a nurturing environment for Jamaican dons to embed themselves in garrisons as governance figures. In Jamaica as well as in other developing countries in the Caribbean and Latin America, the prominence of non-state (criminal and otherwise) actors intensified as states adjusted and, in many cases, scaled back health, education and community development programmes and more general efforts to improve the overall economic and social security of their citizens. Rowden (2009), among other scholars (Giroux 2008; Davis 2007), has referred to the 1980s as the "lost decade" during which the policies of privatisation, liberalisation, deregulation, and budget cuts had disastrous effects on the political economies of developing countries. Neoliberal reforms led to "stagnation or decline in GDP growth, an increase in unemployment, a drop in wages, reductions in public expenditure on social services, and an aggravation of poverty" (78). Many developing countries suffered from declining economic growth rates during this heyday of neoliberal claims. Across developing regions of the globe, GDP and per capita incomes fell by 6.6 and 16 per cent from 1980 to 1988 (78). Developing states in the Americas and on the continent of Africa took heavy economic blows from stagnating growth in those same years.

Jake Johnston and Juan Montecino (2011), analysts associated with The Centre for Economic and Policy Research (CEPR), have pointed out that from 1992 to 2010 in Jamaica, "the exceedingly large debt burden has effectively crowded out most other public expenditure" (4). They have argued that the nation's service debt-related expenditures during the 1990s into 2010 impeded capital investment in education and infrastructure. It also had a negative effect, they conclude, on growth in "human capital". Based on information they provide, in 1991–1992, Jamaica's total public debt (external and domestic) stood at 194 per cent of its GDP; this number declined to 125 per cent in 2002–2003 and stood at 129 per cent in 2009–2010 (3).

The neoliberal order made it more difficult for political party leaders in Jamaica to provide state largesse to their constituents in local communities (Sives 2002; 2010). Neoliberalism resulted in an even greater marginalisation of the poor, working and 'under classes.' Deregulation of markets, privatisation, and the hollowing out of the welfare state resulted in increased social exclusion of the poor; it enriched the bourgeoisie and capitalist classes while wreaking economic hardship on those at the margins of society (Davis 2007; Harvey 2005). This was the situation in the 1980s and 1990s in many countries in the developing world, including Jamaica (Arias 2006). It is within this context that dons (mega and some area) assumed both increased and a greater variety of social, economic, and political roles in their garrisons, moving from being solely party agents to serving as community welfare and social security providers to inner-city residents hardest hit by the new political economic order. The neoliberal turn produced the "governance voids" these dons filled. Arias (2006) has observed that international debt crises and structural adjustment programmes have forced many countries in the developing world to scale back on the social services they provide, especially to urban residents. In addition, governments find it fiscally difficult under neoliberal policies to train police and security officials to deal with the challenges of criminality that have accompanied globalisation (Arias 2006, 11–14).

Neoliberal globalisation has also resulted in the addition of new transnational actors in state governance. As Mark Bevir (2010) has posited, governance has reframed the state not as a unified entity, but as a complex arrangement of interacting networks (62). Neoliberalism creates significant security, health care, education, employment, and social welfare voids. Briquet and Favarel-Garrigues (2010) and Arias (2006) have examined the environments in which criminal non-state actors can emerge and embed themselves as parallel and in some cases alternate sources of governance in Jamaica's garrisons.

Garrison Spaces

This section focuses on the garrison; that is, its infrastructure and socio-economic and cultural character. Describing the Jamaican garrison helps one to understand better some of the factors that facilitated the embedding of dons as governance figures. These neighbourhoods emerged out of a political as well as a socio-cultural context in which members of the urban working class (both employed and unemployed) exist on the margins of Jamaican society (Johnson and Soeters 2008). These communities arose from the development of large-scale affordable housing projects (apartments) provided by the political elite through the state. Residents in these communities as early as the 1970s received homes because of their partisan alliances (Chevannes 1992; Witter 1992). The Report of the National Committee on Political Tribalism (The Kerr Report) described Jamaica's garrisons in the following way:

> The hard-core garrison communities exhibit an element of autonomy in that they are a state within a state. The Jamaican state has no authority or power, except in so far as its forces are able to invade in the form of police and military raids. In the core, garrison disputes have been settled, matters tried, offenders sentenced and punished, all without reference to the institutions of the Jamaican state. (6–7)

These communities are characterised by urban blight, high rates of unemployment, poverty, high homicide rates and violence related to polarised political identities/loyalties and ongoing gang warfare.

Extreme poverty and violence are two dominant features of the garrison environment. Aldrie Henry-Lee (2005) has studied closely the extent and character of poverty in Jamaica's garrison communities. She has argued that garrisons are characterised by high levels of both "private and public poverty", defined as people's ability to enjoy a certain standard of living (private poverty) and as the geographical infrastructure related to housing, sanitation, and public utilities (public poverty). Henry-Lee has presented both dimensions of poverty as defining factors that predispose garrison communities to the influence of dons. She used data from the Planning Institute of Jamaica: *Jamaica Survey of Living Conditions* (JSLC), for the years 1992, 1996 and 2001 to support her claims. Based on this information Henry-Lee pointed out that although poverty declined in the overall Kingston Metropolitan Area (KMA) from 18.8 per cent to 15.0 per cent and then to 7.6 per cent in 2001, the quality of life of garrison residents did not improve. She contends:

> The living conditions of some of the people in most of the 'tribalised' communities' reek of abandonment and neglect ... problems of poor waste management, inconsistent electricity supplies and abandoned structures; these abandoned structures provide some evidence that people leave during outbreaks of violence. (94–95)

This noted analyst approaches the question of poverty in a multi-faceted way. She explored the public and private poverty of garrisons in several parts of Kingston and St Andrew, where she found that residents had low levels of the "essentials" that Amartya Sen (1999) has outlined are critical to basic human subsistence. Henry-Lee tied the level of private and public poverty in the garrison communities she examined in part to the roles played by and the influence of dons within them. In assessing the standards of living of garrison residents Henry-Lee pointed out:

> Their quality of life depends on their degree of social capital that they enjoy with the don ... the residents' movements in and out of the communities and their access to the social goods considered valuable in society, are based on the closeness of their links to the don. (96)

Similarly, Sen (1999) has examined how geographical, human, material and psychological factors affect the level of poverty in urban areas. He has posited that a condition of poverty is characterised by a lack of basic resources and opportunities. He argues that income alone is not a sufficient indicator of poverty because poverty has the effect of reducing the developmental capabilities of citizens. For Sen, the following are essential necessities to ameliorate poverty:

- Acquisition of sufficient food and clothing
- Freedom from ill health, ill-treatment, and disease
- Access to a good education
- Social inclusion
- Participation in community life
- Employment. (87–90)

Chapter four explores the issue of poverty in the garrison environment and provides data on employment and the physical infrastructure of Brown Villa. The primary analytic point in that chapter is that the deep and sustained poverty that has characterised Jamaica's garrisons has helped to legitimise the roles dons play in helping residents to survive. Garrison poverty facilitated the embedding of dons.

Violence, Drugs, and Gun Trafficking in the Caribbean

Another dominant feature of the garrison environment is violence. Different scholars (e.g., Harriott 2004; Lacey 1977; Levy 1996) have observed that fighting related to gang warfare, homicides, jungle justice (local community system of punishment and discipline) and politically motivated conflicts are consistent features of garrison life. Anthony Harriott (2002, 2004, 2008) has observed that Jamaican garrisons are "high violence" communities and that this characteristic manifests itself in their frequency of homicides and multiple mass murders. Henry-Lee (2005) has contended, meanwhile, that violence in garrisons negatively influences residents' capabilities to lift themselves out of poverty. Similarly, the Kerr Report (1997) highlighted how violence in garrisons affects both private and public poverty by arguing that border wars between garrison communities affect law and order, disable social infrastructure (roads, water, garbage disposal, utilities, and supermarkets), restrict human movement to jobs and employment opportunities and preclude businesses and capital investment in these neighbourhoods (6).

Violence, like any physical act of inflicting injury, involves both bodily and psychological trauma. Acts of aggression are often identified with certain geographic areas (Vigil 2003). Caroline Moser and Cathy McIlwaine (2001) have analysed the perceptions of working-class residents concerning urban life in Guatemala. They conducted focus group interviews in nine urban and poor communities and found that residents in each place perceived violence to be the most pressing problem they faced. These scholars reported that robberies and gang wars were the top two sources of violence in the communities they examined (26–27). Violence, particularly among youth, according to Moser and Bernice von Bronkhorst (1999), has four "interrelated levels of causality, structural, institutional, interpersonal and individual" (9). At the "individual level," a lack of life skills and low self-esteem were catalysts of youth-related violence. At the "interpersonal level," inadequate parenting strategies and the overall poor socio-economic status of the family unit were responsible for youth engaging in violent activities/associations. Moser and von Bronkhorst also suggested that low levels of access to quality education and skills training are identified with youth violence in the LAC region. Additionally, they argued that violence-prone neighbourhoods and the absence of employment opportunities in these areas were key factors behind the high incidence of violence in the region.

Policing strategies, which citizens often perceived as predatory, and a lack of trust among residents in the system of justice also encourage violence. At the structural level, the influence of the media, a 'culture' that legitimises violence (especially among young men) and years of social exclusion and inequality are also triggers of violence in the region (Moser and Bronkhorst 1999, 9–16). The field data collected in Brown Villa (chapters four and five) supports the analysis offered by these authors. This work goes a step further, however, by arguing that these factors in the Jamaican garrison context have facilitated the anchorage of dons/gangs. The overall environment in garrison spaces (in this case Brown Villa) fostered the rise and subsequent embedding of dons as despotic governing actors whom residents both love and fear.

In the specific Caribbean context, community violence has structural roots related to colonial history and, in the Jamaican case, as outlined above, a polarised partisan culture. Within the region, as Moser and Bronkhorst (1999) have argued, violence is also the result of the area's developing socio-economic status. Economic inequality, high levels of poverty and communities affected by social exclusion, government neglect of social welfare, housing and education often result in the emergence and escalation of violence and organised crime (Headley 1994, 2002; Harriott, 2008). In a later work, Moser (2006) indicated that after the 1970s, with the influence of neo-Marxist theories of dependency, scholars began to recognise that violence is affected by institutional and structural factors. Using evidence from Latin America, Moser concluded, "inequality and exclusion (unequal access to employment, education, health, and physical infrastructure) intersect with poverty to precipitate violence" (4). Moser's work demonstrates that at least in the context of Latin American developing countries, violence is the outcome of multiple influences, which are often associated with political and economic disputes over turf, and the distribution of resources. Developing states in the region, for example, have a weak record in protecting the lives and property of citizens. Moser (2006) identified economic violence related to extortion rackets, perpetuated by criminal gangs, as a growing problem in Latin America. This reality is also true for the Caribbean. In specific reference to Jamaica, Harriott has observed:

> Violence is a business. It is organised and marketed to yield a regular return as in the case of extortion and protection rackets. Violence brings social success. Violence validates and elevates status. Violence brings political success. It may be used to acquire and consolidate political power as 'safe seats' in the parliament. It has therefore become self-perpetuating. (2009, 5)

The UNDP report (2012) pointed out that violence related to high homicide rates, transnational organised crime and drug trafficking threatens the human security and future development goals of countries in the Caribbean region, "prior to the 1990s, the homicide rates within the region were below the global average. By 1990 however, Latin America and the Caribbean had an average homicide rate of 22.9 per

100,000 citizens and the region was ranked first in the homicide rate among regions of the world" (21). The United Nations Office on Drugs and Crime (UNOC 2005) and the World Bank (2007) have reported that the Caribbean as a region ranked first in the world for homicide rates (30 per 100,000); the South/West Africa region ranked second with a homicide rate of 29 per 100,000 and South America ranked third with 26 per 100,000. Jamaica's homicide rate has routinely ranked in the top five countries of the world (UNOC, 2010). The UNDP report (2012) revealed that in 2009, Jamaica's homicide rate was approximately 62 per 100,000, and in 2010, it declined to about 50 per 100,000 citizens (21). The high rate of violent crime, especially homicides, has led regional scholars such as Harriott (2008), to conclude that there is a sub-culture of violence in the Caribbean, especially in Jamaica. He contends that this phenomenon manifests itself in six ways:

- High rate of homicidal violence
- An affinity for guns
- Predatory and conflict-related violence
- Hypersensitivity to insults (especially among gang members/dons)
- Revenge seeking/retaliatory violence and overt violence/killings in plain sight. (29–36)

This subculture of violence perspective suggests that it is a normative mode of behaviour for criminal groups to endorse and condone such behaviour (Wolgang and Ferracuti, 1967).

Gunst (1996) has examined how Jamaican dons and gangs in the 1970s and 1980s carried out acts of violence related to political partisan contests between the PNP and the JLP. She has also investigated the role of dons in inter-gang rivalries over drug trafficking between cities in the United States and Jamaica. She tells the story of one Jamaican don, "Chinaman", from a PNP garrison, McGregor Gully. "Chinaman" used the revenue from his drug running in the US to "buy clothing, Walkmans (portable cassette recorders), VCRs and guns for the McGregor Gully sufferers" (Gunst 1996, 186). She noted further that "Chinaman" said the guns he sent to his community in Jamaica were "vote getters". They were also useful to "Gully residents" to protect themselves against rival garrison gangs and the police (186). According to reports from the Jamaica Constabulary Force (JCF), Harriott (2004, 2008 and 2009) and the Jamaican *Gleaner,* the availability of guns in Jamaica is linked to the easy access to US markets for small firearms. The UNDP report (2012) blames the trafficking of narcotics across the Americas, and the weak capacity of governments in the Caribbean region to secure their borders for the widespread availability of illegal weapons.

Drug trafficking is a transnational activity that runs along the fault lines of the world's political economy connecting producer, transit, and consumer zones. Drugs, according to Paul Gootenberg (2009), are "psychoactive substances and commodities that for a variety of reasons since 1900 have been constructed as health and or societal dangers by modern states, medical authorities and regulatory cultures". Gootenberg argues that drugs (heroin, cocaine, marijuana, opium, LSD, ecstasy, and methamphetamine) are commercialised products and trafficking in these substances often challenges the effective regulation of Caribbean states' borders. Three main drug trade routes exist in the LAC region: Western Colombia to Central America and Mexico, Mexico into the United States, and Colombia to Jamaica to the Bahamas and into the US. The main transhipment points for cocaine, marijuana and small arms through the Caribbean are Puerto Rico, the Bahamas and Jamaica (Tulchin and Espach 2000).

The Caribbean is a crucial geographic corridor for the United States "war on drugs" because it is the "transit zone" between South America and North America. Scott H. Decker and Margaret Townsend Chapman (2008) maintain that the Caribbean is "an important area for understanding drug smuggling because of its proximity to source and destination countries as well as its long history as a site for smuggling illegal goods and for piracy" (45). A 2008 UNOC study reported that despite successful interception measures, the Caribbean remains a competitive corridor for drug trafficking and gunrunning. The region remains an important site for smuggling because of its historical, language, commercial and tourist ties to consumer countries to the North. Central America [Colombia especially] and Mexico are the dominant drug-running players in the Americas. The Caribbean corridor nonetheless is still active and important to "producer" state traffickers from Colombia, Peru, and Bolivia. In 2005, drug traffickers transhipped an estimated ten tons of cocaine through Jamaica, with twenty tons moving through Haiti and the Dominican Republic. As a recent Report of the International Narcotics Control Board (INCB) observed, "drug trafficking organisations have increased their operations in Central America and the Caribbean, posing a serious threat to human security and affecting everyday life, in the region" (2011, 51). Drug trafficking in Central America and the Caribbean has contributed to the high levels of homicide, youth violence and drug-related corruption of national criminal justice systems in countries in that region (51–55).

Along with a long history of illegal transhipment and piracy, Caribbean nations have small and unstable economies that offer opportunities for drug trafficking to take root. Harriott (2009) has observed that the rise in the "commercialisation of crime" and its transnational and organised nature has facilitated the "development of an illegal opportunity structure that extends beyond our (Jamaica's) national borders" (33). Griffith (1999) has argued that drugs in the Caribbean involve the varied dynamics of production, consumption, money laundering and corruption. In his view, the region offers an ideal geography and geology in which drugs (marijuana and cocaine) can be cultivated and transhipped. Clandestine narcotic operations are possible because of the sea routes that connect the various islands of the region, and the hilly terrain of some countries, including Jamaica, which facilitates the growing of marijuana, often goes undetected by law enforcement authorities.

Biko Agozino et al. (2009) have suggested there is a relationship between the drug trade and gun trafficking in the West Indies. Drugs and guns have a "systemic link", and in the Caribbean and Latin America, "firearms appear to follow drug shipments both large and small along established seaborne routes; in such instances, they are mostly brandished in the context of protecting illicit economic transactions" (294). Laurie Gunst (1995) has analysed how Jamaican posses (gangs) and their dons smuggled and sold drugs on the streets of major US cities in the 1980s. According to Gunst, they (dons/gangs) used the money they made from selling crack, heroin, and ganja to buy assault weapons, including AK-47s, the Israeli-made Uzi and other handguns. Dons and gang members sent these weapons home to their Jamaican garrisons to ensure that upon their return from overseas, they had a "safe place" from rival gangs/dons. The case of "Chinaman" and the McGregor Gully garrison illustrates this "systemic" nexus between drugs and gun crimes.

One key entry point through which guns and drugs enter the Caribbean is via the sea trade routes. Agozino, et al. (2009) have highlighted the existence of drugs for guns trading among Caribbean nations. The authors posited, "There are also inter-island transit links fostered by small fishing boatmen. The islands of Haiti and Jamaica are reportedly linked in this fashion with Jamaican fishermen meeting in open waters close to neighbouring Haiti to exchange drugs for AK47s" (295). This trade involves the exchange of Jamaican-grown marijuana (ganja) for guns from Haiti. When the Haitian army was disbanded in 2004, its streets and towns became awash with assault rifles and handguns. Jamaican fishermen took ganja to Haiti in exchange for these weapons, which they then sold to gangs back home, especially in the urban areas of Montego Bay, Kingston, St Andrew, Clarendon, and St Catherine. The *Gleaner* has published several articles regarding the illicit sea route connection between Haiti and Jamaica. According to one *Gleaner* report, "two thousand and sixty-two pounds of compressed ganja, a 30-foot go-fast boat and two-boat engines" were seized in a joint operation between the United Nations Security Forces and the Operation Kingfish unit of the Jamaica Constabulary Force (JCF), on June 12, 2009 (*Gleaner* 2009).[11] A senior official in the Operation Kingfish unit, according to the *Gleaner* report, "said the operation may have prevented more than 200 illegal guns and thousands of rounds of ammunition from entering Jamaica, as approximately seven pounds of ganja could be exchanged for a gun" (*Gleaner* June 12, 2009).[22] Nick Davis, in a BBC report entitled, *Haiti and Jamaica's Deadly Trade*, noted the security threat that the guns-for-drugs trade poses for Haiti and Jamaica he stated:

> Police say marijuana has traditionally been destined for markets in the US and Europe but increasingly traffickers are heading to

---

1.   Article can be retrieved from http://jamaica-gleaner.com/gleaner/20090612/lead/lead9.html
2.   Ibid.

> Haiti where they trade weed for guns, a valuable commodity on
> the streets of Kingston. 'The trade between Jamaica and Haiti is
> very significant,' says Glenmore Hinds, Assistant Commissioner of
> Police. 'The firearms that come from Haiti are mainly handguns,
> revolvers, pistols and a few shotguns.[33] (BBC 2008)

These marijuana and cocaine "pick-ups" and "drops", whether on
land or by water routes, involve the exchange of guns, drugs, and money.
The drugs-for-guns trade between Jamaica and Haiti came up in this
research during the interviews I conducted with police personnel. In
addition, on a visit to a fishing village in the parish of St Catherine, a
local fisherman who told stories of how drugs and guns enter the island
of Jamaica via trips boatmen make to Haiti. The influence of drug/gun
trafficking on the roles dons have assumed in garrisons, investigated in
chapter five expounds on this nexus.

Drugs and guns have served to empower dons/gangs in garrisons.
Notably, these two are important, but not the only sources of income
to which garrison leaders have access. Political contracts, racketeering
schemes, extortion, and contract killings are other means by which they
finance themselves. Gunst (1996), in *Born Fi Dead: A Journey Through
the Jamaican Posse Underworld*, has argued that by the 1980s, Jamaica's
partisan political culture collided with the emergence of a drug and
gun culture in the nation's garrisons. Dons and their posses became
powerful figures in the Jamaican criminal underworld, which had very
significant international associations.

This chapter has reviewed the relevant academic literature on
Jamaican dons and garrison communities. It also examined relevant
works on governance. I argued that governance as a theoretical construct
considers discourses on the role of the state, the influence of neoliberal
globalisation on governmental policies and the impact that non-state
actors have within and across national borders. The nation-state in the
global neoliberal era, beginning in the late 1970s, began to play a steering
role in the affairs of public governance. The Caribbean literature,
however, pays limited attention to the influence of criminal actors on
the processes and structures of governance. *Don Dada* addresses this

---

3.   A copy of the report is retrievable at http://news.bbc.co.uk/2/hi/americas/7684983.
      stm. The BBC published the account online on 25 October 2008.

gap in the literature by exploring the influence and roles that non-state criminal actors such as Jamaica's dons have within the borders of the nation-state. The literature suggests that governance is multi-level in character and the case of Brown Villa provides a localised example of how individuals (dons) and groups (gangs) gained and sustained control over people, resources, and spaces.

With the Jamaican government's determined May 2010 Incursion into Tivoli Gardens to apprehend and extradite its mega don, Christopher "Dudus" Coke, a dis-embedding process began. Several dons and gangs were dismantled and arrested by law enforcement; however, this decline in the status and social power of dons was temporary. In 2012, the Jamaica Constabulary Force (JCF) reported an increase in violence and homicides related to conflicts between rival dons and gangs. Reports from the JCF and the Ministry of National Security indicate that at the end of 2019, there were 389 active gangs across the island with over two-thirds operating in the Kingston and metro areas in the parishes of St Andrew and St Catherine.[4] If law enforcement and policymakers in Jamaica intend to dismantle gangs, and restore social order and control, they must first understand how garrisons[5] function and the "place" dons have in them.

FOUR

Brown Villa: The Jamaican Garrison Context

Introduction

The first section of this chapter describes the social and economic environment of Brown Villa. It examines the community's demographic composition and residents' education, employment, income, and training levels as well as their perceptions of safety. The socio-economic status and demographic features of residents in Brown Villa represent an important finding as the garrison environment helps us to contextualise the predisposition of its residents, especially those under age 25, to behaviours of dependency, delinquency, and the adulation of dons. The second half of the chapter, examines the central challenges that affect residents in Brown Villa.

Garrison residents confront daily a range of challenges, including high levels of poverty and unemployment. Charting those concerns provides a lens into the political, economic, and social context in which dons have emerged and entrenched themselves. This section relies on information from the Social Development Commission (SDC) Community Profile 2011[1] for Brown Villa as well as interviews with individuals who live or work in the community. The SDC Community Profile outlines the main demographic, employment, and educational features of Brown Villa. The SDC report noted six major developmental challenges the neighbourhood's residents identified as critical in 2007 and 2011. Figure 4.1 tracks the shift in concerns among residents over time regarding the pressing challenges their community faces. Insecurity from crime and violence was a major concern in 2007, while high unemployment, especially among youth, is a serious developmental challenge the community continues to confront (SDC 2011, 59).

Figure 4.1: Brown Villa Residents' Perception of Community Challenges 2007 and 2011

(Numbers are Percentages)

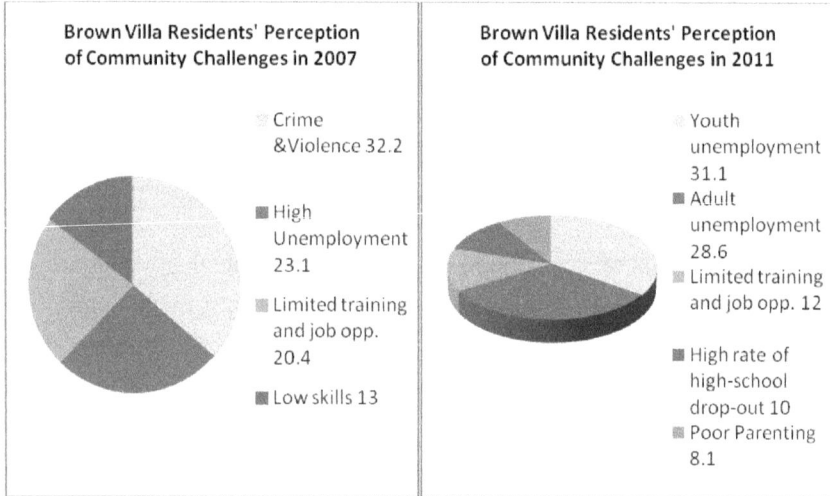

Brown Villa Residents' Perception of Community Challenges in 2007	Brown Villa Residents' Perception of Community Challenges in 2011
Crime &Violence 32.2	Youth unemployment 31.1
High Unemployment 23.1	Adult unemployment 28.6
Limited training and job opp. 20.4	Limited training and job opp. 12
Low skills 13	High rate of high-school drop-out 10
	Poor Parenting 8.1

Source: SDC Community Profile, Brown Villa 2011

Amartya Sen (1999) has argued that the lack of certain basic resources contributes to poverty and hinders development. These critical attributes or elements, including access to good education and employment, are in short supply in Jamaica's garrisons generally, and in Brown Villa particularly.

Socio-economic Status

Demography: The community is a youthful one, with the bulk of the population between 10 and 30 years old and more than 62 per cent of the population under 30. A large percentage of residents are children under the age of 15. Along with limited state-sponsored social services, relatively high dropout rates from school for a small community, poor parenting skills and supervision, the "youthfulness" of the garrison environment is an ideal location for non-state actors, including criminal types such as dons, to emerge and embed themselves in the life of the community. A police officer from the Community Policing Unit in Brown Villa, pointed out in an interview, for example, that "dons use the

Table 4.1: Age and Sex of Brown Villa Residents 2011

Age Cohort (yrs.)	Percentage Male	Percentage Female	Percentage Total
0-4	4.9	4.4	9.3
5-9	6.0	5.6	11.6
10-14	6.5	6.2	12.7
15-19	6.6	5.6	12.0
20-24	4.2	4.7	8.9
25-29	3.4	4.4	7.8
30-34	2.3	4.2	6.5
35-39	2.3	3.2	5.5
40-44	2.8	3.6	6.4
50-54	1.7	2.1	3.8
55-59	1.7	1.2	2.9
60-64	0.7	1.0	1.7
64+	2.1	2.9	5
Total	**47.4**	**52.6**	**100**

Source: SDC Community Profile 2011 (13)

community, especially its high schools, as recruiting grounds for gang membership" (VT009 Interview, September 16, 2011). Dons emerge in these contexts due to these communities' diminished stock of political trust in the state, low levels of human capital and limited employment opportunities. Garrisons also evidence, as several interviewees observed, low self-esteem among residents (Henry-Lee 2005). The poor quality of education and training and low-income levels of residents are specific manifestations of poverty and of a more generalised dearth of economic development at the macro level in Jamaica.

Education and Training: According to the 2011 SDC report, 74.5 per cent of Brown Villa's household heads have no academic qualifications, that is, no high school diploma or post-secondary training. A mere 2.8 per cent possessed an associate degree or post-secondary professional qualification (5–6). The SDC data also indicated that 9.8 per cent of household heads had at least some vocational training, while only 5.1 per cent of them had passed one or more subjects at the Caribbean Examinations Council (CXC) General or General Certificate of Education (GCE) 'O' Level.[2] SDC data reveal that 62.7 per cent of other household members had no academic qualification (that is, no official certification in a field of study). Interviewees noted the neighbourhood's limited educational opportunities and frequently poor quality of secondary schooling as a major problem in the garrison.

Employment and Income: Sixty-six per cent of Brown Villa household heads were employed in 2007. This figure dropped to 55.2 per cent in 2011. The 2011 SDC survey found 38.5 per cent employment, with 64.1 per cent of the labour force in Brown Villa aged 14 to 64 unemployed (37–45). The unemployment rate, based on the 2011 survey, was highest (21.2 per cent) among those aged 20–24, and it was higher among women. Thus, unemployment, especially among younger people, is a serious problem in the Brown Villa garrison. The SDC has reported similar figures in other metropolitan areas in the nation. For the entire country, the Statistical Institute of Jamaica (STATIN) reported a 25.7 per cent unemployment rate for the age group 20–24 in October 2010; this figure rose to 27.4 per cent in the following year.[3]

Among household heads in Brown Villa, 46.5 per cent earned less than JM\$30,000 (equivalent to US\$350) per month (SDC 2011, 38).[4] This income level places them in poverty. These data capture income only for those classified as 'household heads.' Income from other members may also be a factor in the overall income level of the entire household. On average, residents live on less than US\$11 a day (calculated in the first quarter of 2012 USD to JMD exchange rate). These data echo Henry-Lee's (2005) analysis of the levels of private and public poverty in garrison communities. She argued that while poverty levels declined in the KMA between 1989 and 2001, the quality of life of the residents living there did not improve. Such seems to be the continuing reality for Brown Villa residents.

Violence and Community Safety

Nearly two-thirds of SDC report respondents in March 2011 suggested it was unlikely they would be a crime victim in the next 12 months, while 14 per cent said it was likely and 7.9 per cent suggested it was "impossible" (53). In the interviews conducted for this work, respondents who live and work in Brown Villa and similar garrison communities observed that since the May 2010 incursion into Tivoli

Table 4.2: Major Public Safety Threats in Brown Villa

Public Safety Issues	Percentage
Gangs And Gang Warfare	20.5
Overgrown Lots	11.0
Derelict Buildings	9.5
Raw Sewage in the Streets	13.1
No Streetlights	4.2
Inadequate Street Lights	15.2
Inadequate Disposal of Solid Waste	15.7
Failed Infrastructure	13.4
None	41.5

Source: SDC 2011 Community Profile (54)

Gardens, their communities felt safer. The Jamaica Constabulary Force (JCF) and the Jamaica Defence Force (JDF) have since stepped up policing operations by targeting garrison gangs and dons in many urban inner cities in the KMA. Interviewees (residents of Brown Villa and Tivoli Gardens) did point out, however, that before Coke's arrest, they experienced periods of violence in their communities related to gang warfare, including reprisal killings and sexual assaults. It is possible that a general drop in the crime rate in the country in late 2010 and early 2011 influenced SDC respondent perceptions in March 2011.

Interviwee residents of Brown Villa and neighbouring communities, when asked individuals to share their perceptions of their community's safety early in the interview, spoke cautiously and reservedly. Later in the interview, however, these respondents tended to speak more openly and freely about the nature of the problems, they had experienced. According to Brown Villa residents, these concerns included drive-by shootings by rival community gangs, firebombing of their homes as acts of reprisal and the restriction of their movement across community borders into neighbouring town centres. Table 4.2 suggests that despite the relatively "safe" perception respondents reported to the SDC concerning daily life in Brown Villa, they nonetheless also shared several perceived major continuing threats to public safety. Gang warfare was residents' top concern linked to public safety.

The failure of the Jamaican state and private businesses to provide services such as health care, decent housing, and proper training for garrison residents to take advantage of employment opportunities created openings for dons to emerge and for them to play several social roles. STATIN has reported that between 2006 and 2009 an average of 176,000 persons were employed for the first three quarters of each year.[5] Many garrison residents do not qualify to have access to employment in these industries named by STATIN.

Garrison residents perceive dons as "ghetto governors who help them to survive" (Interview, September 16, 2011: VT011) given this reality. Residents view some dons as providers, protectors, arbiters of social justice and facilitators of their economic survival. Meanwhile, they view others, particularly street dons, as predators who extort from the community and sexually oppress residents, especially young women. The interviews conducted suggested strongly that garrison daily life exposes residents (the young in particular) to violent behaviours and gang cultures. Residents, police, and NGO/CBO interviewees pointed out that poor parenting values and a lack of social trust for those considered outsiders to the realities of garrison life characterise these communities. This cultural/sociological analysis is important as it helps interested observers to understand the material and non-material factors that prompt residents to support or reject dons' governing roles.

The challenges that garrison residents face highlight, on one level, the weak capacity of the Jamaican state. Residents look to dons as alternative sources for economic survival, leadership, and security. Charles Tilly (2007) has suggested that when state capacity is low, democratic governments are threatened by "higher involvement of semi-legal and illegal actors in public politics" (20). Since its colonial beginnings in the 1930s with the formation of trade unions and political parties, the Jamaican state has never enjoyed a strong economic base. When Jamaica became independent in 1962, local political leaders confronted a growing and restive poor urban and rural working class since the economy was too small to provide jobs and entrepreneurial opportunities to most of the nation's newly independent citizens. The largely agriculture-based economy depended on foreign importation of locally produced sugar, citrus, and bananas. Jamaica also offered bauxite as part of its externally driven export economy.

By 1970, Jamaica was almost completely reliant on foreign trade and had become an import-dependent economy. This situation had its roots in

Figure 4.2: Theme 1: Problems Facing Garrison Residents

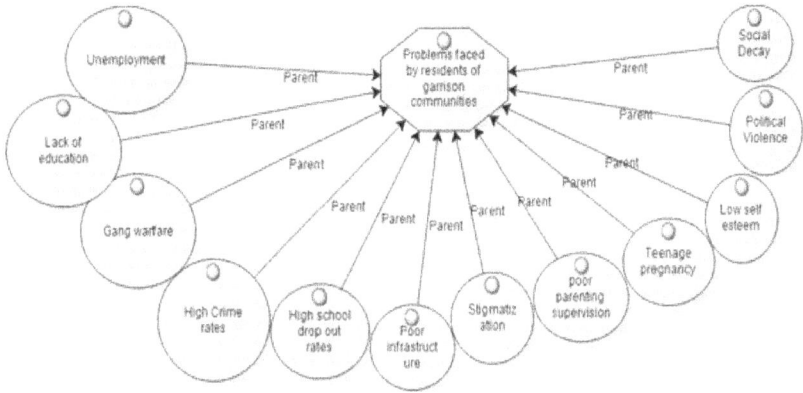

Produced from interviewees' responses to the question, "What are the main challenges faced by residents in garrisons?" Figure generated using NVIVO; the size of bubbles indicates the frequency and ranking of problem as identified by interviewees.

the nation's colonial history of dependence on Britain. George Beckford (1972) has argued that it is third-world economies such as Jamaica's inherited plantation-based economies that have contributed to their conditions of 'persistent poverty' and underdevelopment.[6] Interviewee VT014 (an elected representative) recalled that the Jamaican state was unable to provide economic opportunities for its growing urban population in the 1960s and 1970s. By the 1980s, a series of economic crises and the consequent drying up of political contracts and largesse from the government positioned solidified the position of dons in the nation's garrisons. According to VT014, "Dons emerged within the context of weakening political officialdom" (Interview, September 23, 2011). In short, a weak economic base at the macro (state) level is one key factor that facilitated the rise of these criminal actors in Jamaica's garrisons. When there are limited available sources of earning legitimate income and sustainable means of economic survival, people are predisposed to create their own solutions or attach themselves to those that appear able to provide them.

Crisis of Unemployment

Unemployment was a significant and recurrent sub-theme among interviewees who cited a lack of job opportunities as a major problem that affected residents, especially youth in the community. One interviewee (VT021), who has lived in Brown Villa for more than forty years and directs a community-based organisation, maintained that a lack of education and job creation are the two most critical problems garrison residents confront. In his view, dons and gangs would have less influence if residents had greater access to these needs. As he remarked,

> For me what I think is the greatest challenge in this community is education and job creation, because if people had jobs, if people had education, they would know how to control and conduct themselves. Because I've seen people work inside of this community, men who would normally deh pon (be on the) corner as gangsters and dem (they) get a job and dem (their) job is only night job, suh (so) in the days they can only sleep cause (because) them (they are) tired and then at the night they're off to work. So you see where job creation and education can make a difference in these communities. (Interview, October 12, 2011: VT021)

Another interviewee (VT007), a clergyman who has worked in Brown Villa since 1999, leading a non-profit organisation aimed at dispute resolution among rival gangs in troubled inner-city communities, connected unemployment, poor parenting skills and violence in Brown Villa as central social challenges. He remarked:

> Probably the first thing I would say is that the reputation of Brown Villa and the reality are two different things. Often the name of Brown Villa evokes fear, dread, and those kinds of things. There have been and still are some dangerous elements in the community. But the number one challenge is unemployment. A lack of employment, a lack of family cohesiveness, young people growing up finding their way in life at a very, very young age, very little parental supervision and investment, and parents having grown up the same way not having the sense of esteem to invest in their children. So you get all of these problems like teenage pregnancy, high dropout rates in school, and as a result of that, you do have family breakdown, very poor sense of conflict resolution skills and as a result of that, yeah, violence. (Interview, September 6, 2011: VT007)

Later in the interview, VT007 noted that the high levels of unemployment and the stigma of living in a garrison community made basic economic survival difficult for the residents of such neighbourhoods. He opined that there is a basic need for "survival in the community and [that] a general lack of hope" pervades the area, where most people are "trying to do the best they can". Residents have great difficulty getting jobs if it is known their home address is in a garrison neighbourhood. Potential employers tend to fear the perceived criminality popularly associated with garrisons. External stigmatisation of urban inner-city communities by potential employers, state officials, the police and others has often hindered residents' opportunities to obtain legal employment.

The need for youth employment and other opportunities to secure a sense of economic survival came up in most of the community-based organisation representatives' interviews I conducted. According to interviewee VT010, a clergyman who has worked with local and international NGO groups in Brown Villa since 1994, the community needs "alternatives"; "if there is no strong economic base, it can breed crime and violence". Many "idle youths" in the community are not employed, and "when youths are not occupied it leads to problems" (Interview, September 14, 2011: VT 010). There are no branch plants in Brown Villa, and residents are desperate for employment opportunities. In the garrison, the only signs of economic activity were small corner shops and some street vendors who sold their wares (chewing gum and other confectioneries) to students attending neighbourhood high schools. The 2006 Report of the Special Task Force on Crime, *Road Map to a Safe and Secure Jamaica* (Road Map), highlighted the high rates of youth unemployment and social inequality in Jamaica's urban inner cities. The report noted that the high rate of violent crime in Jamaica, especially in garrison neighbourhoods, has its "roots" in this reality of youth unemployment and social inequality. It concluded, "A high proportion of violent crimes are committed by young males who are unemployed and underemployed" (8).

The 64.1 per cent youth unemployment rate of Brown Villa, when viewed in the context of the Road Map's analysis, provides a picture of the relationship between unemployment and criminality. A former "foot soldier"[7] to a don (Interviewee VT027), who lives in one of the districts of Brown Villa, decried the functions played by the Jamaican state in his community in securing basic economic survival among residents. He contended that successive governments have given minimal support to the development of his neighbourhood. In his view, residents support dons because they help people in the community survive during hard times. According to this Interviewee (VT027), a young person who opts to be a member of a don's gang does so most often because of the financial remuneration and social status such a role can bring. It pays to be a worker for the don; it provides an income as well as social power and respect (whether out of fear or adoration) from garrison residents. He contends:

> That is why you always have to have a don in Jamaica; they provide certain things you won't get from the government. They provide a form of safety that the police will not provide. They provide jobs and pay the youths weekly just for being in the thing (gang). They provide a lot of things even though they go about the wrong way doing it". (Interview, October 25, 2011: VT027)

On May 21, 2012, the Jamaican prosecutors who won a court battle to extradite drug kingpin and don of Tivoli Gardens, Christopher "Dudus" Coke, presented a cooperating witness (CW-1) statement to the US Southern District Court of New York. The witness told the court that he was a part of the Shower Posse gang that operated in Jamaica and the US. In his statement, he declared that he served as a bodyguard to Lester Lloyd "Jim Brown" Coke (head of the Shower Posse and Christopher Coke's father) during the 1980s. CW-1's statement highlighted his role in the community and beyond: "I became, in essence, a trusted senior counsellor to the organisation. Jim Brown periodically paid me for my services, in amounts up to 40,000 Jamaican dollars at a time." Interviewees VT027 and CW-1 are examples of scores of young males inside Jamaica's garrison communities who have found employment working for dons.

The *Report of the National Committee on Political Tribalism, 1997* (Kerr Report[8] 1997) described the socio-economic conditions of garrison communities. In its findings, the Committee decried the absence of governmental support, poor sanitation, and high unemployment in these inner-city areas:

> The slum communities around the parish capitals, particularly, Kingston, St Andrew, and St Catherine continue to grow as unemployed and undereducated youths migrate from rural communities in search of a better opportunity...It is very clear that poverty and illiteracy provide the opportunity for politicians to create and nurture political tribalism. (Kerr Report 1997, 15–16)

These conditions have also provided the opportunity for dons to nurture a gangster culture and to organise criminality. Nonetheless, the Kerr Report did not pay specific attention to dons. Anthony Harriott (2008) has contended that violence in Jamaica's urban communities is attributable to three factors: economic strain and the rate of youth unemployment; social disadvantage and inequality; and the ineffectiveness of the criminal justice system (53–63). Caroline Moser, Bernice von Bronkhorst and the World Bank (1999) have suggested that institutional factors such as one's neighbourhood environment contribute to the escalation of youth violence and their membership in gangs. Moser et al. have explored the potential root causes of youth violence in Latin America and the Caribbean and concluded that economic and cultural factors predispose inner-city young people to violence and organised criminal organisations. The interview findings indicate that there is indeed a strong link between youth unemployment, the overall garrison social environment and gang violence in Brown Villa. The influence of dons is a part of this association; residents (especially those aged 14 to 30) often receive employment opportunities from dons. VT032, who sits on the executive board of several CBOs that provide social services in garrison communities, summed up the link between unemployment and the power/role(s) of dons.[9] Asked if it was possible to diminish the power of dons in garrisons, he responded:

> It's possible and it's one thing that can get rid of the dons; economics. If everybody in a community can get a job then they will not need anyone to do anything for them. It is simple, simple economics. Whatever label you want put it under, economics is the bottom line because if people are not able to gain employment, then the don won't go out of business. (Interview, November 9, 2011: VT032)

The Scourge of Gang Violence

Interviewees frequently emphasised the presence of gang warfare in garrisons. In the 2011 SDC report, residents named gang warfare as the major threat to their sense of public safety. Community-based interviewees lamented the many lives lost because of gang feuds over turf, reprisal killings and politically motivated violence. A gang emerged in the 1990s in one of Brown Villa's districts, for example, when a group of young men decided to avenge the deaths of their fathers, killed during the turbulent politically motivated wars of the 1970s and early 1980s. This gang, according to a police interviewee (VT018), remains involved in violence related to robberies, extortion, murders, turf wars, shootings, and reprisal killings in the community.

Those interviewed noted the evolution of gang warfare in Jamaica's garrisons. They uniformly reported that such violence during the 1970s was politically motivated and typically erupted over partisan differences. However, by the early 1980s, with the introduction of cocaine transhipment between Colombia and Jamaica, the character of gang violence shifted into battles over drugs and gun trafficking. Laurie Gunst (1995) has demonstrated how drug and gun trafficking within and beyond the borders of Jamaica influenced gang violence in Kingston. Jamaican posses fought on the streets of New York and Miami in the 1980s over which would control what areas of turf for drug sales. The streets of Kingston and its surrounding region overflowed with guns and gangs thereafter, in part because of the wealth Jamaican dons acquired in North America.[10] As McKinley reported (1990) in the *New York Times*:

> For a decade, the gang of illegal aliens from Jamaica, known as the Gulleymen, operated a network of crack houses and heroin dealers that at its high point took in more than $60,000 a day in profits, agents with the Federal Bureau of Investigation said. The profits went into real estate in Brooklyn and on Long Island or were shipped back to Jamaica, some to boost the campaign war chests of Jamaican politicians, the agents said.[11] (McKinley 1990)

Violence linked to partisan identities and gangs continued during the 1970s and 1980s. However, by the late 1980s and early 1990s, politically motivated violence had begun to decline. This decrease is attributed to a rise in organised crime and a gradual process of separation between party officials and dons. Most interviewees (35 of the 42) maintained that after 1980 or thereabouts, garrison dons and gangs gained wealth and power via their participation in illicit international trade in guns and drugs, rather than principally through patronage from political leaders.

By the late 1990s and early 2000s, gang warfare began to occur over turf linked to drug sales and partisan identity inside garrison communities. A divisional ground commander from the Brown Villa police department (JCF) argued in an interview that the major gangs in the area and other adjoining communities have political-partisan identities that sometimes filter into conflicts over territory and the ascension to power of dons (October 4, 2011: VT018). The acquisition and control of swaths of urban territory have material benefits for dons as they use garrison communities (their "safe zones") to carry out illicit activities clandestinely, including car theft and gun and drug trafficking.

A major gang war erupted during the mid-1990s between the leading posse in Brown Villa and that of a neighbouring garrison. Every interviewee that lived or worked in the community (residents/police/NGO) discussed this conflict in their interviews. The violence arose in part because of deeply divided partisan loyalties between JLP and PNP sympathisers, and in part from turf battles. Interviewee VT015, a resident of Brown Villa for more than 30 years and a member of a local youth social intervention CBO in the area recounted what she experienced during the crisis. She became very emotional as she pointed out that the dust-up arose when a don from a neighbouring community wanted to annex parts of Brown Villa to increase his geographic control. She lamented,

> I would never want to experience anything like that again, not ever. Persons were forced to do things and say things to each other. I don't want to go back to when that was happening. It was awful to see how people were treated like animals. It wasn't police who were dealing with people like that; it was civilian to civilian, don to don. (Interview, September 28, 2011: VT015)

Another interviewee, who also lives in Brown Villa and administers an early childhood basic school (kindergarten), discussed the connection between turf and politically motivated gang violence. She also addressed the inter-community war of the mid-1990s and observed that local gang members and the don in her community provided security and protection against the "invasion" of the opposing don and his posse from an adjacent community. According to VT011, "This was a four-year war; people were killed along the border, in the downtown marketplace, and at bus stops. ... It was hell. Children got killed and old people in wheelchairs got killed" (Interview, September 16, 2011: VT011). She noted further that the don in her neighbourhood sent his foot soldiers to collect money to buy bullets to protect the community. When asked if the area's residents collaborated with the don and gang members, VT011 responded: "You give the money because you know it's for a worthy cause. Even though you know it will kill women and children. It's really for a worthy cause" (Interview, September 16, 2011).[12]

Gun Culture and Violence

Guns are important to the power and control dons exercise in garrison areas.[13] Dons and their foot soldiers use guns to protect turf, commit crimes that bring in revenue to pay gang members and provide some social services to residents of their home garrisons. Figure 4.3 shows the high use of guns in Jamaica's homicides.

A "gun culture," based on interview responses from NGO directors, journalists, and senior police officers, first took root in the nation's garrisons in the 1970s when politicians began to issue guns to their political enforcers to maintain partisan power in the urban enclaves of Kingston and St Andrew. With the trafficking of drugs and guns in the 1980s to and from the United Kingdom and the United States, dons began to buy their own weapons, and it was that turn that caused state legislators to begin to lose control over the borders of garrison communities. A senior officer, Senior Superintendent of Police (VT022) in the police division in which Brown Villa is located, pointed out in an interview that 28 gangs currently operate in the 16 communities that make up the division. He noted that the two main posses in the detachment's jurisdiction each have alliances with either the Jamaica Labour Party or the Peoples National Party. He suggested that both gangs have surrogate (smaller, affiliated) posses also operating in the division, observing: "The choice of weapons used by these gangs are rifles, the M16 and AK 47s; some gangs use pistols, revolvers and the two major gangs are equipped with rifle grenades" (Interview October 12, 2011: VT022).

Table 4.3 provides an overview of the agents of homicides in Jamaica during 2009, 2010, and 2011. The graphic suggests that a high percentage of the nation's murders during the sample period were gang-related. Gang-related murders fell in 2010, due in part to the government's sustained efforts to remove and prosecute dons following its May 2010 extradition of Dudus Coke. Figure 4.3 supports interviewees' claims that dons and gangs use the "gun" disproportionately to extend their power and control in garrison communities.

Table 4.3: Murders by Type, 2009–2011

Context (Murder Assessment)	2011		2010		2009	
	Reported	% Rep	Reported	% Rep	Reported	% Rep
Gang Related	553	49.2%	398	27.6%	882	52.4%
Domestic	101	9.0%	59	4.1%	69	4.1%
Criminal (Not Gang)	380	33.8%	592	41.1%	642	38.1%
Mob Killing	14	1.2%	0	0.0%	0	0.0%
Not yet established	77	6.8%	393	27.3%	90	5.3%
Total	**1125**	**100%**	**1442**	**100%**	**1683**	**100%**

Source: Jamaica Constabulary Force (JCF) http://www.jcf.gov.jm/crime-stats

Figure 4.3: Weapons Used in Murders in 2011

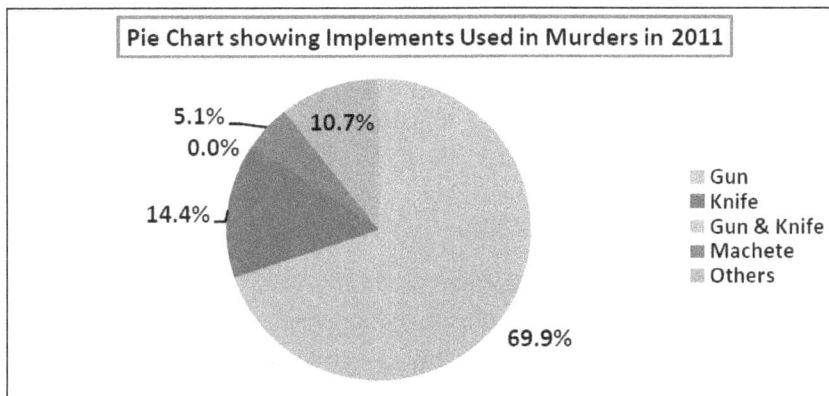

Source: Jamaica Constabulary Force website at http://www.jcf.gov.jm/crime-stats

Limited Educational Skills and Training

Of the 26 community-based persons (NGO/CBO/ residents/clergy/ police) interviewed in Brown Villa, 20 pointed out that limited opportunities for education and training are closely associated with the high unemployment rates in garrison communities such as Brown Villa. The high rate of youth unemployment in garrisons facilitates their dependence on partisan and non-state actors for job opportunities.

According to the SDC Report 2011, Brown Villa youth aged 14–24 accounted for "9.7 per cent of the total percentage of employed household members, which was below the national youth employment rate of 14.6%" in 2007 (2011, 41). The *Kerr Report 1997* points out that the low educational and skill levels of garrison youth make them prime targets for partisan manipulation. According to the Report, "jobs are regularly tied to political affiliation. The sources of work are also limited by the high concentration of persons who have no skills and therefore form part of a very large group of common labourers" (16). What the Report did not mention was that dons routinely distribute government jobs in garrison communities. Elected representatives channel construction, drain cleaning, garbage disposal and landscaping contracts through garrison dons, who in turn give selected residents access to these posts. In describing the ongoing symbiosis between elected representatives and dons in providing employment opportunities to unskilled/under-educated residents in garrisons, Interviewee VT005 (a journalist) observed:

> There needs to be a way to share the spoils. Now the person that emerges as the area leader, the community leader, or don is the person who shares the spoils. There is no way the economic benefits can be thrown on the ground and everybody just grabs what they want, there is no order. There has to be someone he (elected representative) delegates to. Therein comes the emergence of what we've begun to call a don. (Interview, August 11, 2011)

The low level of skills and education in garrison communities facilitates the embedded status of dons and their performance of governing functions. Frances Madden (2011) summed up the impact that the socio-economic environment of garrisons has on residents' choices to get involved in illicit activities.[14] She has argued that given the harsh economic realities, many garrison residents aspire to migrate to the US or the United Kingdom, which residents refer to as "foreign" for a better life. Those who decide to remain inside the garrison engage in buying and selling "both legal and illegal goods" (8). She went further to point out that young women in garrisons engage in relationships with older "dominant" males for financial gain. Some young men according to Madden "saw access to a gun as an option for power and economic gain as exemplified by those who had gone this route (such as the "don") and who appeared to have gained social mobility (8).

Dons, particularly mega dons and to a lesser extent area don types, fill the vacuum left by the Jamaican state in garrison communities by providing residents with assistance in health care, employment, housing, education, and skills training. They also make drug trafficking opportunities available to those interested and thereby entry into the Jamaican criminal underworld. Table 4.4 shows the qualification of household heads for occupations in construction, beauty care, machine, and appliance, secretarial, clerical, professional /technical skills, computing, and information technology in Brown Villa. Only 9.8 per cent of household heads had training in professional/technical skills, while 1.3 per cent had training in computing and information technology. The highest proportion of those with training, 16.6 per cent, were skilled in the provision of beauty care and related services (hairdressing, barbering) (SDC 2011, 23–24).

Moreover, such occupation training as is available is often informal in character. Table 4.5 shows that 57.6 per cent of household heads received training informally without certification.

The challenges of high unemployment and limited access to education and training, coupled with poor housing and sanitation, contribute to poverty and under-development in Jamaica's garrisons. They also produce, as the data show, volatile communities characterised by periods of high insecurity. Taken together, these factors suggest that the garrison environment serves as a catalyst for dons to embed themselves in these communities and play several welfare, security, and quasi-judicial roles.

Table 4.4: Qualification/Training by Gender in Brown Villa 2011

Training Received	Sex of Household Head		Total
	% Male	% Female	
Beauty care and services	1.8	14.8	16.6
Secretarial and office clerks	1.3	3.6	4.9
Hospitality skills	4.1	11.9	16.1
Art and Craft	3.6	.8	4.4
Construction and Cabinet making skills	13.7	0.0	13.7
Machine and appliance	10.1	1.3	11.4
Computing & Information Technology	0.5	0.8	1.3
Apparel and sewn product skills	2.3	13.2	15.5
Commercial and sales skills	0.0	0.3	0.3
Professional and technical skills	6.2	3.6	9.8
Agriculture/farming	1.0.	0.0.	1.0
Other Skills	3.9.	0.5	4.4
Skills not stated	0.3	0.3	0.5
Total	49.0	51.0	100.0

Source: SDC Report 2011(24)

Table 4.5: Level of Training/Qualification for Household Heads in Brown Villa 2011

Training Qualifications	Percentage
Learn from more experienced person	37.2
On the Job	20.4
Professional or Technical: With certificate	10.2
Professional or Technical: Without Certificate	3.2
Vocational: with certificate	19.0
Vocational: without certificate	10.0

Source: SDC Report 2011 (24)

FIVE

Violent Entrepreneurs: From Partisan Puppets to Don Dadas

Introduction

A process of transformation in the don's roles began to occur beginning in the 1980s. This shift, influenced by global economic factors as well as national changes in development policies, created several transnational non-state actors such as the don in the Jamaican case and the drug cartels in the South American countries of Colombia, Peru, and Bolivia. These new participants were involved in illicit markets and other criminal activities and were or became members of organised criminal groups. This chapter argues that dons are now governing actors embedded in Jamaica's garrison communities. The roles performed by dons vary based on whether they are of the mega, area or street don type. Each type of don wields power in specific ways.

Dons perform four central functions in garrison communities. They provide: community welfare; security and protection; partisan mobilisation/enforcement, and law, order, and conflict resolution via "jungle justice" measures. These are social, political, and economic functions. Jamaican dons derive their popularity, power, and legitimacy from their capacities to deliver material and immaterial "goods" to garrison residents. Figure 5.1 depicts the major roles dons perform in garrisons. In wrestling with the concept of "donmanship", it is necessary to differentiate and classify these leaders. The interview responses by Brown Villa residents suggested that not all dons behave in the same manner and that a garrison community could have different types of dons over time and across its geographic terrain of streets and districts. To address this finding, a typology was developed to describe the varying roles different dons perform in garrisons. For example, some interviewees who live in Brown Villa observed that the don (Don

"Z" – a street type) in their district provided few community welfare services. However, he did offer security and protection and community members reported feeling safe from robberies and external attacks from neighbouring garrison gangs because of the presence of the don and his foot soldiers. Chapter one introduced a tripartite classification of dons:

- **Mega dons** perform a wide range of roles in the garrison because of their access to large sums of money, resources, personnel, and a stockpile of weapons. These individuals exercise influence and power across different garrisons and have strong connections to local and international businesses (both legitimate and criminal).

- **Area dons** also play a range of roles in their communities, but these leaders do not have the strong transnational links that mega dons evidence. Area dons usually control a specific garrison and they often report to a mega don. Brown Villa has had two such dons (Dons "X" and "Y") from the 1990s to the present.

- **Street dons** are lower-level community leaders. These individuals control a street or streets in a garrison community. Interviewees indicated that several street dons might function in a single garrison. Street dons typically have limited resources (money) and very few guns at their disposal. Since they do not possess large resources, they are not as well equipped to perform welfare roles in their communities, as are area or mega dons.

Figure 5.1: Interviewees' Description of Roles Dons Play in Garrisons

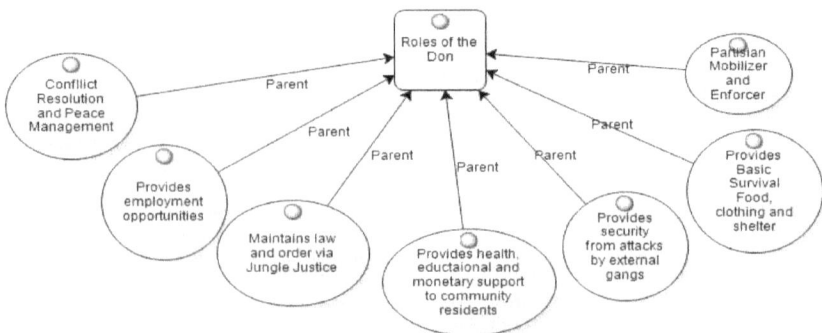

Social Power and the Functions of Dons

Community Welfare: The community welfare role that dons perform sheds light on the low capacity (Tilly 2007) and/or willingness of the Jamaican state and private businesses to provide for the economic security of citizens residing in garrisons. This role relates to the contribution dons make to the physical infrastructure of the community as well as to the household well-being and economic survival of residents. As already noted, unemployment is a serious problem in Brown Villa. Interviewees (especially clergy, NGO/CBO members) suggested that most garrison residents are constantly engaged in a search for ways to improve their economic status. Not trusting elected officials to assist them in such efforts, citizens often turn to dons as alternate sources of welfare provision. At the household level, interviewees noted that some individuals receive cash assistance from dons to buy food, and the elderly often receive funds to purchase medication. Mega dons offer this kind of support routinely. In Brown Villa, there is evidence of one of its area dons performing such roles too. Interviewee VT024, a garrison resident and clergywoman, remarked that in the community:

> You may have an old lady that might be diabetic or have high blood pressure, when she goes to the doctor and come home with a prescription, she will go and look for him (the don) and explain that she does not have the money to pay for her medication. The don will go into his own pocket and pay the cost. (Interview, October 20, 2011)

All categories of respondents observed that some dons provide employment opportunities to garrison residents and financial support to families, especially to mothers to send their children to school. Interviewee VT004, an NGO director who works in several inner-city Jamaican communities, described how residents become dependent on a don to help them take care of themselves and their families:

> There is no legitimate source of supplying basic needs, the state has failed, and you have an economic structure that creates this dependency on the don. If you have two sons and you have no breakfast to give them, if you walk over to the don and say my kids have no food to eat, he will say ok, go over to the supermarket and

get some bread and things for your kids. You then are thankful to this guy because he allows your family to eat; when the police come to arrest him for any charge you don't testify against him because you know you will need bread and butter another day. (Interview, August 30, 2011: VT004)

Rattray (2001) has argued that dons are by-products of Jamaica's weak economy and the influence of its polarised partisan culture. I have echoed that argument above. Referring to one of Kingston's reputed mega dons, Donald "Zekes" Phipps, Rattray sketched the social welfare roles that residents associate with dons. Rattray described a 1998 protest in downtown Kingston staged by residents from the community in which Zekes was the don who took to the streets to protest the leader's arrest by JCF police officers; four persons including two police officers were killed in the altercation. Rattray summarised this dynamic of the power, social function, and assent among residents of the mega don Zekes in the following way:

Unabashed demonstrators praised his magnanimity. They openly related how he fed, sheltered, and protected them. They said that he schooled their children and did for them what the security forces and the politicians were either unable or unwilling to do. However, nobody broached the taboo topic of the source of the great wealth needed to feed, clothe, school and protect most of the downtown community.[1] (Rattray 2001)

In his article, Rattray revealed and questioned the sources of funding that dons use to build their gang networks, purchase weapons and make monetary and other contributions to garrison residents. Table 5.6 details the various strategies that dons use to accumulate money, weapons, and other material resources. How dons use drug trafficking and other criminal and non-criminal means to acquire wealth and build their capacities to perform different socio-economic and political functions in garrisons is examined later in this chapter.

According to JCF reports, Zekes had a lucrative criminal empire that involved drug trafficking and robberies. He was reported to have been the mastermind behind extortion rackets in the Downtown Kingston business districts and public transportation networks (bus parks and taxi services) in the late 1990s. Zekes and Christopher "Dudus" Coke are examples of mega dons – their wealth and influence over several geographic areas in the KMA were unparalleled in the 1990s and 2000s.

Not all dons, however, are willing or able to perform the community welfare role. A clergyman who has lived in Brown Villa for more than thirty years and who runs a CBO in one of the community's districts, pointed out that the don in the area (Don Z – street type) in which his organisation operates is very rich. However, he does not provide any welfare services to the community or its residents. Instead, that individual employs force and violence to maintain his control over "his" territory in the community (Interview October 11, 2011: VT020). Based on information gathered from residents, this individual purchased his donmanship from another more powerful mega don. He had very little support among community members given his reluctance to engage in distributive services. His decision to provide minimal social welfare assistance to his district, even though he had the capacity to do so, indicates that dons' personalities may influence how they choose to define their social roles. While a psychological assessment of dons was not an objective of this book, future research on the psychological profile of Jamaican dons could profitably focus on these concerns.

Dons use both force and material resources to secure the support of garrison residents and to establish themselves as "legitimate" holders of authority and power. Interviewee VT001, a journalist, described how dons use the proceeds from narcotics trafficking to embed themselves in garrisons by providing needed services:

> With the retreat of the state and the vacuum created, yeah, the don acted as an economic player/stakeholder. He did so not out of any goodwill for the community but for personal selfish economic reasons, he was benefiting handsomely from the illegal drug trade, the illegal guns and ammunition trade, the illicit contraband trade. Yeah! Those activities generated millions of dollars for them. They were then able to use that source of economic wealth to supplant the politician in respect of buying the loyalty and support of community members who were largely unemployed, underemployed or unemployable. They were able to support them, to ensure that children got lunch money, school fees were paid, and food was on the table through the drug link. (Interview, July 26, 2011: VT001)

As a general proposition, providing social benefits to their garrison communities is particularly important to mega and area dons as the garrison provides them with a necessary base for their broader criminal enterprises.

In several interviews with residents from Brown Villa, I asked what dons wanted with these communities. I asked why gangs engaged in bitter battles over spaces that seem to have very little to offer. Garrison neighbourhoods are poor communities, with little infrastructure in the form of housing stock, public buildings, and business office space. For example, according to the 2011 SDC Report, there is only one financial institution in Brown Villa. On visits to the community, I observed that the public buildings, schools, the police station, and the community centres were in desperate need of repair. The neighbourhood reflects Aldrie Henry-Lee's (2005) neatly descriptive condition of "public poverty". NGO leaders, journalists, and senior police interviewees confirmed that similar situations exist in other garrison communities in Jamaica.

Dons assist residents and attend to the community's welfare as a means of integrating themselves into the social and cultural fabric of the community. Christmas and Easter treats, for example, have cultural significance in Jamaica, and dons recognise this tradition. These celebrations have taken root within the context of a Jamaican environment that embraces Christian mores and values. European colonisers transplanted these celebrations to the Americas under the system of plantation slavery and colonisation from the seventeenth to the nineteenth centuries. During plantation enslavement, Christmas celebrations (food and entertainment) were important markers of communal dignity and belonging among enslaved Africans. At Christmas time in particular, slaves were allowed time off from the rigours of plantation work – labouring from dusk until dawn planting and harvesting sugar cane. In the post-emancipation period after 1838, Christmas celebrations remained and intensified as culturally entrenched activities in Jamaica. Of the 42 interviews undertaken, 18 interviewees (clergy, CBO members, and residents) praised dons for promoting a positive "vibe" in the community through Christmas and

Easter gift-giving, supporting public concerts, and hosting dances and other amusements for the garrison's children.

Community street dances, for example, constitute a culturally significant activity that dons provide for garrison residents. Community members dress in the latest dancehall[2] clothing, dance and enjoy popular melodies. Dancehall music and its accompanying street concerts and exotic dress are important features of the cultural make-up of garrison communities. This genre of music also has significant appeal in wider Jamaican society. Public street dances in garrisons also provide employment and other economic opportunities to residents. When dons host these events, residents can sell wares such as alcohol, cigarettes, gum and other confectioneries. Males from the community get jobs providing security and young women often serve as bartenders. A journalist (VT005) noted that some dons self-consciously use the proceeds from street dances to contribute to the welfare and development of garrison communities. Area and mega dons also use such events as a means of laundering drug money, directing some of the profits to host "back to school," Christmas and Easter treats.

Residents develop a dependent economic relationship with their mega and area dons, and they learn, as one interviewee noted, "not to bite the hand that feeds them" (Interview, November 17, 2011: VT033). This finding supports James Montgomery's (1998) analysis, who has argued that social actors learn to "calculate trust" with each other based on roles performed. The don-to- garrison-resident relationship evidence a bond of trust, one held together in large part by people's desire to ensure their economic survival in conditions of urban squalor. Interviewee VT024, a clergywoman, commented that residents frequently develop an attachment to their community dons out of economic necessity. She said that dons provide garrison residents with a sense of communal belonging and well-being, in addition to material assistance. In her neighbourhood, the don hosts gatherings for the distribution of the Christmas and Easter community treats for residents. At these events, children and adults are entertained and receive gifts and food items, all courtesy of the don's patronage. VT024 described the ways in which the don in her community attends to resident welfare:

In this community and not only this community, they have
Christmas treats where they would get things, get the children out
there and they would give them ice cream, give them a little doll.
For back-to-school treats, if you as a mother have five kids going
back to school, school fee, lunch money, the bags, the books, so
forth, and you know that this man is keeping a treat you can send
your kids and they come home with a bag, a few books, and a few
pencils. You have young people who would say I want to start up a
small business, but they don't have the money, the don would say
ok, I will give you a start. He (don) put a 5,000 JA$ dollars (U.S.
$60) in the hands of the youngster so they can start a business.
People in the community view this man (don) as a king; he cannot
do any wrong in their eyes. (Interview, October 10, 2011: VT024)

Brown Villa residents consistently pointed out in interviews that
dons provide families with school materials for their children, such
as composition notebooks, pens, pencils, and even money to pay
tuition and fees. Whatever else might be said of the perhaps cynical
underpinnings of such gifts, these forms of support also indicate that
some dons at least, recognise the importance of education to the future
development of garrison youth. In one interview, a resident (VT015)
explained that some street dons in her community ensure that young
children go to school, sometimes by use of force. She also suggested
that in her garrison, dons often chastise children who skip classes.

In short, however mixed their motives, dons perform governing roles
in their communities. Providing opportunities for human development
through educational access has the potential to improve the living
conditions of people in garrison areas. This is an accepted function of
government and governance. Some dons, based on the views of several
interviewees (residents, police and NGO respondents), also contribute
to the infrastructural development of their communities (for example,
road repair, and construction of community walls). VT015 summarised
some of the governance-related services that dons provide in her district
of Brown Villa:

In short, however mixed their motives, dons perform governing roles

Not all dons want to tear down the community, some of them want
to build it because they know they have their kids and families
there. A few dons now are into development, they build up places
(for example, local grocery stores) and get youth employed; who

can cook the don will say ok go to HEART[3] and get a certificate in training in cooking and he will pay for the certificate. If the wall in the community needs fixing, they (dons) will do it and not wait on anyone to come do it. They host fundraising events (such as street dances) and use some of the proceeds to fix the wall. (Interview, September 28, 2011: VT015)

Early in the interview, Interviewee VT015 (resident/CBO member) noted that not all dons contribute to their communities. Some leaders, including many street dons, are simply fiscally incapable of doing so, while others are less altruistically inclined as individuals. This is the case for the street don "Z", alluded to above. Some dons simply do not regard it as their role to offer welfare services of any sort. Street dons carry out sporadic robberies to take care of themselves and their corner crews (loosely organised small gangs). They are not involved in organised crime, such as drug trafficking or large-scale extortion rackets, so they have limited resources to offer residents in the territories they control in garrisons.

Street dons tend to use violence and intimidation against garrison residents more frequently than area and mega dons as a means of signalling their authority. Providing social services is not the foundation of their power in the community. Instead, they gain support and assent from garrison residents principally for the security and protection roles they perform during periods of inter and intra-garrison conflicts between/among rival gangs. Interviewee VT015 shed light on the mixture of fear and goods-and-services provision that street dons use to establish and maintain their power in garrisons. When asked how these leaders manage to remain in good stead with residents, despite having little economic patronage to offer, Interviewee VT015 explained that these types of dons operate,

Sometimes not by force directly, but some of the parents like when their children are with don(s), so they defend them because she [child] gets to go to school and money comes into the household, even if he breaks the daughter's hand she has to stay with him (don) because that's how the money comes into the household. So you will find that sometimes they [dons] drive fear into residents, even when the people do not want them, they drive fear. (Interview, September 28, 2011: VT015)

Two leaders in Brown Villa, classified as area dons ("X" and "Y"), had tremendous influence across the five districts of the community, and both enjoyed the loyal support of at least some street-level dons. Both individuals operated in the community from the 1990s into the 2000s. However, one is now dead, and the other has lost much of his influence to street dons. Each of these dons operated differently in Brown Villa. One had a stronger welfare approach to the community. He gave financial support to several residents and sponsored community-based projects (sports, entertainment, and the building of recreational parks). The other don was more interested in building his cocaine business. He supported his foot soldiers and close associates and showed little interest in providing community-oriented services or activities. Interviewee VT007 commented on the differences between the two men,

> There are some dons who are very much doing things for their own interests and there are some who are geared towards community; one dealt with cocaine primarily. He had some legitimate businesses, he had a wholesale up there, he had a couple of legitimate businesses, but it was well known that he would sell cocaine in the area. (Interview, September 6, 2011: VT007)

Dons, depending on the type and their personal predilections, perform welfare tasks that help residents survive the often-harsh economic realities of garrison life. The interview data indicate that the more resources a don has and the stronger his association with the international illicit drug market, the more likely it is that he will possess the capacity to offer services and make welfare contributions. Whether they do so, however, also appears to depend on their psychological orientation, personal calculus, and proclivity. To put it succinctly, in Jamaican garrisons, mega and area dons often perform this sort of governing role, but street dons appear to do so to a far lesser extent.

Table 5.1: Dons' Sources of Wealth and Weapons by Type

Don by Type	Strategy of Resource Accumulation (Weapons & Money)
Mega Dons	• International illicit markets (drug/gun trafficking) • Local illicit markets (drugs/guns/contraband such as cigarettes • Local legal markets (entertainment/construction/retailing) • Government Contracts • Extortion Rackets (Large businesses—supermarkets) • Mega Robberies (banks) • Contract Killings
Area Dons	• Local illicit markets (drug--marijuana based/contraband) • Local legal markets (entertainment/construction/retailing) • Government Contracts • Extortion Rackets of Transportation systems (buses/taxis) • Contract Killings • Gun renting • International remittance and gun smuggling from overseas contacts
Street Dons	• Robberies on city transport systems (buses/taxis) • Sporadic extortion inside home garrison • Robberies of other urban and sub-urban communities • Contract Killings • Working for Mega or Area Dons • Extortion of small businesses in the metro-area • International remittance

Security and Protection: Residents associate dons with security and protection. All residents interviewed as well as several police and NGO members argued that dons provide garrison inhabitants protection against external threats through their gangs/crews. Brown Villa has a long history of violence and insecurity related to partisan conflicts and battles between rival gangs. As early as the 1970s, residents in the community suffered from politically motivated shootings, arson, and violence linked to reprisal killings by gangs from neighbouring garrisons.

Violence also occurs among rival gangs over turf and power inside the community. In most cases, these gangs battle over drug (marijuana and cocaine) distribution and business districts where they extort, while in other cases, the conflict may arise from interpersonal tiffs between contending dons or gang members (Levy 2009; Madden 2011). Violence takes place in households as well. All female residents interviewed noted that dons sometimes have defended them against domestic violence and abusive men. Community interviewees (15 residents/CBO members) indicated that dons' provision of security and protection represents an important role they perform in garrisons. Residents trust their dons to protect their personal property from robbery and arson and to provide security from the externally generated violence perpetrated by rival dons/gangs. Interviewee VT011 explained that dons:

> Protect the community; what I mean by protection is that sometimes you have internal war in the community or war from other communities. They protect the community from men who will come in to kill, rape, or whatever in the community. (Interview, September 16, 2011: VT011)

In short, dons and their gangs fill the vacuum left by the Jamaican state in the arena of security and they operate as local "police" or "militia" forces in their neighbourhoods.

An Amnesty International Report on violence and insecurity in Jamaica's inner cities, notes that "the worst violence was reported during clashes between rival gangs for control of communities and territory. During these confrontations, the entire population is held hostage, literally shut in by barricades" (2008, 5). Under such conditions, schools are closed, residents are prevented from going to their jobs, and obtaining access to health care is difficult. One resident, a former member of a gang during the 1970s, described how he, under the orders of a don, fought to protect a section of Brown Villa during the politically violent period of the late 1970s. According to interviewee VT042, the don he worked for allowed the "community to stay alive and survive, we had to hold off men from neighbouring rival communities, it was a matter of survival against the invasion of these politically motivated paramilitary groups" (Interview, December 5, 2011: VT042). In describing garrison violence in the late 1970s, he said "every day you see gunshots and dead bodies. I lost many friends in the 1970s … many people lost their lives during this time over politics. … In those days people died left, right and centre, it was very bad" (Interview, VT042). While these intense political wars are no longer taking place inside Brown Villa, 16 of the 26 community-based interviewees suggested that periods of extreme gun violence among disparate dons and gangs persist. In addition, political identities continue to contribute to such acts of gang and don violence.

Streets in Brown Villa are blocked with junk cars, logs, and refrigerators. Interviewees point out that this was a security strategy administered by dons. Gang members are ordered to use such debris as defence measures against drive-by shootings and reprisal attacks from rival gangs. By protecting their garrison communities from external attacks, dons help to promote internal peace. In three interview sessions, residents agreed that one of Brown Villa's dons provides few community services. However, they argued that because of the don and his gang, the community has experienced a period of internal security and protection from rival garrison posses since 2000. This buffer against attacks and threats to the community's security comes at a cost as dons use extreme violence to maintain control. Interviewee VT020, a clergyman who has lived in the community for more than 30 years and now administers a local social intervention association, noted, "We have a good relationship with the dons and gangs. They look out for us, they protect us." Later in the interview, however, as he got more comfortable talking about the issue of dons and gangs, he observed:

> In *district name omitted*, was… is a very oppressive structure … although for the past 10 to 12 years, people on the outside you know, will tell you that *district name* has been the most peaceful community. From where I sit, I think that donmanship and what that represents is probably the most devastating thing that this community has to deal with. … No question about it. (Interview, October 11, 2011: VT020)

Such a view suggests that residents often make calculated decisions to accept the collateral damage that comes with the security and protection that dons provide. There was a similar response in another district of Brown Villa. A resident (VT011) there suggested that during an inter-community war (the same event that another community respondent mentioned above), street dons played important roles in safeguarding the community from reprisal killings and attacks from a neighbouring garrison don and his foot soldiers. The interviewee later remarked, "Some dons are by force, sometimes the people don't like them [dons], but it's by fear because they (dons) kill the most people; they are callous, so people fear them; they get power by fear" (Interview, September 16, 2011). The use of oppressive measures and fearmongering are essential for many dons to maintain their positions of dominance inside garrison neighbourhoods. Interviewee VT011 offered that some public displays of support for dons are a result of fear. This view is consistent with those suggested by the police, NGO/CBO officials and journalists. VT011 argued,

> People have to pretend like they like them (dons) because sometimes you see residents go and protest and pretend like they like them; you think they want to do it? They don't want to do it. It's because of fear. (Interview, September 16, 2011: VT011)

Along with the fear that residents have for dons/gangs, they also appear to develop a survivor's trust for those informal criminal leaders who promote their human security. In periods of conflict, or when there is a threat of loss of their personal properties such as cell phones, money and or home appliances (radio, television, or laptop), garrison residents often rely on their area dons for protection and support.

Thirty-one of forty-two interviewees (residents, CBO/NGO officials, journalists, academics and one retired police officer) observed that excessive use of force by the police and their unwillingness to patrol garrison neighbourhoods have reduced residents' trust and confidence in the JCF to protect them. A police officer in charge of the Community Policing Unit in Brown Villa remarked that residents perceive the police to be "the enemy" and that only the don can "create a safe haven in the community" (Interview, September 16, 2011: VT009). He noted that before the May 2010 Incursion into Tivoli Gardens and the resultant increase in police patrols in KMA garrisons, residents seldom gave the constabulary information about violent crimes, robberies, and domestic violence or gang rivalries. Another police interviewee, VT022, argued that the constabulary suffers from labour and resource constraints in carrying out their duties. In his view, to provide security for garrison residents against gang attacks, drive-by shootings, and reprisal killings,

> You would have to establish a police force inside there; you would have to have a police presence on every street to get the type of trust that is required from residents. Yeah, because in truth and in fact the police is not able to give them that sort of security. If a rival gang /don enter the community the police is not always there to respond. (Interview, October 12, 2012: VT022)

Perceived corruption within the police force adds to residents' distrust of the law enforcement agency. Herman Goldstein (1977) views police corruption as the misuse and manipulation by police officers of their authority for personal desires (188). These aspirations range between the material and the immaterial such as power and status. In the Caribbean context, specifically in relation to Jamaica, Anthony Harriott (2000) has argued that police brutality is one strand of corruption. In his view, viciousness occurs to achieve "socially valued" ends. Harriott offered the following rationale for police excess; "in the face of disrespect from young males or displays of any disregard for police authority, police brutality often becomes an exhibition designed to demonstrate the total power, including the power of life and death" (50). Garrison residents often complain that they receive little respect from the JCK, which provides limited safeguards for their civil rights.

All residents and NGO director interviewees (seventeen individuals in total), one retired policeperson and two senior police interviewees contended there are nefarious links among dons, their foot soldiers, and some members of the police responsible for protection efforts in Brown Villa. Some members of the police force grew up in garrison communities, and so have childhood and communal ties to dons and gang members. One journalist (VT005) suggested why residents are reluctant to invest their trust in the police: "There's an East Kinston don who the rumour was his bodyguards were four members of the police force who follow him to the gym every morning, follow him to the supermarket every day" (Interview, August 11, 2011: VT005). VT035, a resident of Brown Villa for more than 33 years, stated, "Police are not trusted in these communities, well this is changing now, but the police have had deep links with dons. When there is going to be a curfew and raids, the police would call dons beforehand and warn them" (Interview, November 14, 2011: VT035).

In 1993, a National Taskforce on Crime concluded,

> The link between police and the criminal element has resulted in a loss of confidence in the police. Numerous persons appearing at the public fora across the island expressed unwillingness to supply information to the police, as they feared there would be a breach of confidence, which could result in reprisals.[4] (1993, 42)

Similarly, in 2006, another national report on crime and violence, *Road Map to a Safe and Secure Jamaica* noted that residents have low levels of trust in JCF members because of rampant corruption within its ranks. The *Road Map* suggested that corruption within the police force is one of the "roots" of Jamaica's violence and that it facilitates the perpetuation of serious crimes. Some reported corrupt practices of JCF members included "sale of ammunition, advising criminals of planned police interdiction, planting and stealing evidence, providing bodyguard service for dons and contract killings or 'murder for hire'" (8). In this view, police corruption facilitates an environment of insecurity, often leaving citizens with limited choices concerning whom to trust to protect them. As VT024 (resident and clergywoman) reported, people in the garrison,

> Support the system that they feel is protecting them. Because we know that everybody have a right to life, the right of everyone to protect themself in whatever they can and the majority of the people in the garrison are not able to protect themself so if there is a system by which they feel protected then they are going to support that system and that's how the dons get their glory. (Interview, October 20, 2011: VT024)

Security is an essential function of the state. Several theorists of democracy (Barber, 1984; Nozick, 1974; Rawls, 1971; Sandel, 1996) contend that the state's central role is to provide protection for its citizens and secure its borders. Scholars have noted that the state in the face of local and global challenges of organised criminality and terrorism is receding in its security roles (Colak and Pearce 2009).

Jungle Justice: Jamaican garrisons operate as de facto shadow states of the official Jamaican state. That is, they constitute "states within the state".[5] Residents often depend on dons and their foot soldiers to provide them with recourse to justice. For them, the state's official law enforcement and court systems seldom guarantee justice. Dons promote order inside "their" garrisons by overseeing local systems of rules and an indigenous judicial system referred to as jungle justice by interviewees. According to the residents of Brown Villa, don-ordered justice is swift and direct, and it prevents individuals or groups from disrupting the social order and stability of the community. Jungle justice, as the name suggests, is a radical local version of law and order. Although perceived as "fair" by residents, it invariably involves violent measures of discipline and punishment. The don, with his council of foot soldiers, is in many instances, the judge, juror, and executor of "justice" in garrisons. Several interviewees, across all categories of respondents, claimed that garrison residents perceive jungle justice to be more accessible, quicker and more results-oriented than that provided by the Jamaican state. It involves strict "rules of engagement" for residents. For example, an unwritten "law" prohibits committing robberies within one's own garrison, disrespecting the elderly or the don, and sexually abusing women in the community unless sanctioned by the don. Interviewee VT005 (a journalist) maintained that dons provide:

> A system of justice which our justice system doesn't provide for so many persons in the inner-city communities. If two persons have a dispute, the don will listen and he will determine that one person was wrong and will decide the punishment. (Interview, August 11, 2011: VT005)

Interviewee VT021, a long-time Brown Villa resident and CBO director, described the thought process that takes place in the mind of a parent whose daughter has been raped. The police will take time to investigate, to ask questions of the rape victim that will likely further traumatise her, and in many cases, the perpetrator will go unprosecuted. The don, on the other hand, usually makes an immediate decision, and he often knows how to find the perpetrator. In the interviewee's words, "jungle justice is swift and sure. You don't go to the police if a man rape your daughter, you just don't. The don can decide the mode of punishment on the spot" (Interview, October 12, 2011: VT021). Actions like these elicit residents' trust and admiration for dons; they know that the official state system will not give them the same alacrity they desire. Whatever its emotional attraction among residents, the danger of this form of "justice" is that it foregoes due process in the name of swift retribution. Several residents, NGO and police interviewees confirmed that people are indeed often wrongly accused and subsequently unfairly punished.

Jungle justice takes place when infractions are committed inside a don's home garrison. In Brown Villa, the police and residents reported that dons set up a kind of judicial "tribunal" that tries people for "crimes" they commit in the community. Different punishments are imposed for different types of crimes: dons order a hand or leg broken for stealing, public beatings with pickaxe sticks (baseball bats) for disrespecting or harming the elderly in the community and the loss of an eye, a gunshot in the foot or even death, for sexual molestation or rape. If a don is disrespected or challenged or a resident becomes a police informant, the punishment is often death, and the person's body is dumped in the open to serve as a public example. A member of the community gets a "road sentence" if they are wanted by the police. This means that they must leave the community until the police investigation is complete, or the person has served the equivalent of their jail time. Such sanctions reduce sporadic visits and raids on the community by the police.

According to Interviewee VT004 (an NGO/CBO director), a "gathering of the brothers to make decisions about the affairs of the community" occurs periodically inside garrison communities (Interview, August 30, 2011: VT004). "Brothers" refers to the don and his top-ranking lieutenants. Dons administer a system of "fowl coop justice" as a strategy of keeping garrisons under their control. Fowl (chicken) coops are common in rural communities of Jamaica; residents in urban areas also use fowl as a means of subsistence for their families. Some city residents also raise chickens for commercial purposes as a modest source of income for their households. Interviewee VT004 noted that in the garrison communities in which she works, dons/gangs often use fowl coops as holding cells for persons who have committed infractions inside the garrison. Such "prisoners" are denied food and water for specified periods, depending on the severity of their "crimes". One resident (VT015) suggested in an interview that if a person steals in the community, they could spend up to two weeks so incarcerated. In Brown Villa, an old sewage treatment building in one of the community's districts serves as the don's makeshift prison. Residents refer to it as the "cell".

Since garrison residents perceive the official state system of law and justice as corrupt and from their perspective ineffective, they have little confidence in it and consequently, use it very little. Data from the Economic and Social Survey of Jamaica (ESSJ) show that between 1999 and 2008, on average Jamaica's police cleared a little more than half of reported cases of carnal abuse and rape each year. In 1999, of all such reported cases, 41 per cent were closed; in 2002, fewer than half (49 per cent) were cleared, and in 2008, the ESSJ reported that police had closed 46 per cent of such investigations. The documents collected and analysed underscored these low rates of success and community perceptions and suggested that Jamaica's judicial system simply is not working adequately. For example, one report (the Road Map for Peace 2006), noted that "justice is a key component for the delivery of governance and the reassurance of the citizenry about the value of equity and fair play. Decay in the system throws governance out of kilter and fosters corruption" (25).

Garrison residents often perceive the judicial system, which includes the police, judges, and the courts, as a "Babylonian system"[6] that treats the poor unfairly and unequally. When they speak of law and order, they are referring to the don's law and order rather than that nominally offered by the state. Jungle justice is another tool used by dons and their foot soldiers to entrench themselves in their communities. In the face of the failure of the police and the state judicial system to act swiftly or to act at all in too many cases, residents frequently feel compelled to use a "system" they perceive listens and will punish those who have wronged them.

At the root then of garrison residents' support of jungle justice is their perception that they are an 'out group' within the larger Jamaican society. They view the official judicial system as one in which they possess, from their point of view, no real stake and in which they will never be treated as equal citizens. Interviewee VT018 (police) observed that the poor urban class in Jamaica will always have limited access to legal redress and justice from the nation because in his view, "The legislators have played with our constitutional rights from time immemorial. … You have to leave it squarely on our legislators. A speedy trial was never embedded in the constitution for the man who can't afford an expensive lawyer" (Interview, October 4, 2011: VT018).

Jungle justice is important to both dons and residents. On the residents' side, it is part of a "system" that they can rely on to protect them, and when necessary, bring those who have wronged them or their families to a local 'court,' for justice to be served. For dons, playing this role allows them to maintain territorial dominance and control in garrisons. A former foot soldier of an area don in Brown Villa (VT027) remarked that through jungle justice, the don sends a signal to residents and other lower-ranking dons that he has the power to punish and discipline anyone who breaks his rules; the interviewee termed these "garrison codes". This role is as much about delivering a perceived service to garrison residents as it is about dons/gangs exacting fear, intimidation and violence against residents and their rivals. Dons/gangs employ jungle justice as a strategy to keep residents in line with garrison codes and dependent on them. Interviewee VT030 (NGO and clergyman) argued that dons sometimes are perceived as "godfather" figures in garrison communities: "They are all-powerful guys who gained their legitimacy in garrisons first from politicians. Every don wants to remain powerful and try to keep people poor to keep them dependent on them for welfare resources and protection" (Interview, October 16, 2011: VT030).

Community-based interviewees (22 in total: police, NGO/CBO and residents) argued that dons help to maintain order and peace in the various districts of Brown Villa. Sociologists, including Emile Durkheim and Karl Mannheim for example, have debated the nature of human societies and the importance of order to the maintenance of cooperative social relations (Wrong 1994). Although jungle justice is often violent, it has become a system in which residents place their confidence. Dons of all types perform this role, and it neatly illustrates their governing capacities to discipline, punish and maintain social order.

Political Mobilisation: Ian Boyne, a renowned Jamaican journalist, remarked that "the links between Jamaican politics and criminality are well established and the transaction costs of these links are incalculable" (*Gleaner* 8 February 2004).[7] He further asserted that both political parties (JLP and PNP) have been guilty of closely embracing political thugs and gunmen to secure electoral victories and intimidate opponents. He pointed to the PNP's embrace of "Burrey Boy" and the JLP's association with "Claude Massop" as specific examples.[8] Commenting on the relationship that dons and partisan actors in Jamaica have developed over the years, interviewee VT0129[9] observed that in the early days of the nation (the 1960s/1970s) the main role of a don was to ensure "political purity, he was the guy who would do the political cleansing" (Interview, September 21, 2011: VT012).

Today, while dons perform this role, they do so to a lesser extent than their predecessors did in the 1960s and 1970s. Ensuring that a particular party had popular support through assent or force was a central function of dons up to the mid-1980s in garrison neighbourhoods. Although they still perform partisan roles in 2012, dons have expanded the range of their social and economic capabilities, as their roles have allowed.

Figure 5.2 depicts the shift in the structure of power and control in garrisons from the pre-to the post-1970s era. Initially, the political class drafted dons into the operational structure of their parties and used them to aid in governing. The relationship started as a patron-client one, with dons being dependent on politicians. However, the association later changed markedly as the social and economic power of dons increased and their augmented power base allowed them to serve as alternative sources of governance for garrison residents.

Figure 5.2: Power Structures in Garrisons, Pre- and Post-1970s

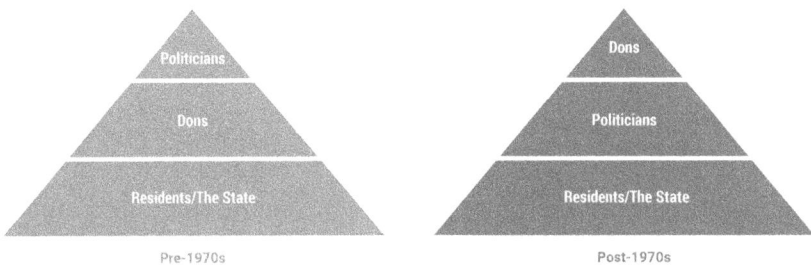

Pre-1970s   Post-1970s

By performing enforcement and mobilisation duties, dons were able to establish their political and economic credentials among partisan actors and with garrison residents. An elected representative who has served in the Jamaican parliament since the late 1970s, Interviewee VT014, observed that dons "secure social legitimation by being of 'value' to political leaders and to their communities" (Interview September 23, 2011: VT014). Dons initially served as vote-getting agents for party officials of the JLP or the PNP, who employed them to ensure electoral victory and the maintenance of political power in Kingston Metropolitan Area constituencies.

By the late 1970s, dons had become important brokers of political and economic services in garrisons and residents perceived them as local arms of the state. The don was the person who possessed the external relationships necessary to bring essential services such as garbage disposal, street cleaning and even unskilled job opportunities to garrisons. Area and mega dons used their political connections not only to assist residents but also to enrich themselves. Interviewee VT004 (an NGO/CBO official) described how elected representatives liaised with dons (area and mega) to ensure their party's popularity and power. Dons,

> Get some money from the Member of Parliament, which is to run the community, so that the streets sweep up and that kind a thing. They get any contracts that come whether through the Solid Waste Agency to clean up and that kind a thing. Remember they are now the community contractor, UDC[10] all those places run (administer) contracts and the foot soldiers are now the main employees because they work for dons and they get cheap pay. (Interview, August 30, 2011)

Previous research (Figueroa 1992; Sives 2002, 2010; Stone 1985) and national reports on crime and violence in Jamaica have cited the relationship between dons and elected officials as one of the primary roots of garrison instability, insecurity, and violence. Dons received weapons to protect turf from partisan rivals and to intimidate residents whose support waivered for the party that controlled their community. The *Gleaner* reported during the 1980 general election, for example, that approximately 800 persons were killed in politically motivated violence.[11] A decade or so thereafter, as noted above, the Wolfe Report observed that the partisan roles dons played in garrison communities routinely contributed to insecurity and violence in those jurisdictions. The Report recommended, "Politicians must not only pay lip service to, but must also become actively involved in the eradication of a political arena where gunslingers establish and operate tribal boundaries" (18). Interviewee VT014 (an elected official) argued that the gun became a feature of political violence in the 1960s. Prior to that time, weapons primarily were sticks, stones and the knife: "It [the gun] became the main vehicle of violent contention and shifted the link with politics and violence" (Interview, September 23, 2011). By 1966, the connection between the nation's political parties and its "rude bwoys (boys)" had solidified. The rude bwoys, largely urban unemployed youths, apathetic and social deviants, my interviewee argued, had moved from being knife carriers to gunslingers.

The latter half of the 1960s to the 1970s was a politically violent and divisive period in Jamaica's history. The same elected official called 1966 the "tipping point" for the escalation of political warfare between communities that supported either the PNP or the JLP. In 1967, Jamaica held its first general parliamentary elections since independence. Chapter 2 noted the rapid development of political gangs across the communities of Kingston as partisan identities radicalised. According to Terry Lacey (1977), "the most important feature of political violence during the 1960s was the development of open political warfare between rival party groups in Kingston in 1966–67" (82). The national government declared a state of emergency in October 1966 because of urban street battles and violence linked to polarised partisanship. VT004 (an NGO/CBO official) suggested to me that the dons and their foot soldiers continue to this day to carry out "door to door" mobilisation and campaigning in garrison areas. They conduct pre-election day audits to assess the party's popularity. The auditing process is dangerous because it is the point at which intimidation takes place, as it requires residents to declare their support for the dominant party in his garrison. On the day of elections, the don and his foot soldiers ensure that people vote for the political candidate that represents whichever party is dominant in that community (Interview August 30, 2011: VT004).

In Brown Villa in the 1970s and 1980s, interviewees recalled a close relationship between the Member of Parliament (MP) and the don of the community. According to an elected representative (VT017):

> The then MP brought a particular style of leadership that I don't think has ever been repeated and a lot of persons want to distance themselves from it. A lot of strong-arm tactics were used, of course, in developing what you have in some of the housing arena and so on. (Interview October 3, 2011)

Frequent reports in the *Gleaner* during the 1970s confirm that violent strategies of forced migration and firebombing homes took place often in Brown Villa and were politically motivated and carried out by the don's foot soldiers. The aim of these atrocities was to ensure that the garrison remained aligned to one party.

This picture began to change in the 1980s as dons became more autonomous and dons began to sponsor and give monetary support to elected officials who wanted to maintain political power within garrisons. Some scholars argue that dons became the new patrons and politicians their new clients in the decades after the 'cocaine explosion' (Rapley 2003; Sives 2002). Indeed, as dons have increased their power inside garrisons, they still partner with elected officials rather than treat them as a client in a patron-client relationship.

Responding to the question, "Are dons, since the 1980s pulling away from their political associations?" Interviewee VT012 (a businessman/ NGO) observed, "It's not that they are pulling themselves from politics, the don was always aware of the importance of political power. They were always aware" (Interview, September 21, 2011: VT012). Interviewee VT008 (resident/CBO) noted that one of Brown Villa's area dons (Don Y) "was a different kind of don, less of an area or community leader; he engaged more in his drug-running business, had cocaine shops in the area, hosted street dances and entertainment" (Interview, September 8, 2011). The interviewee said more about 'Don Y.' What she described reflects the general shift that took place in the power structure of Jamaica's garrisons in the 1990s and 2000s. In her words, "he was more into a flashy lifestyle, 'big cars,' 'big bikes' and had a lot of money to spend on his crew and foot soldiers" (Interview September 8, 2011: VT008).

Carl Stone (1990) has argued that the "one party constituency model" of Jamaica's political parties is destructive to democracy. In his words, "democracy was being raped at gun point" in the garrison constituencies of Kingston and St Andrew during the 1970s and up to the 1980 election as the two main political parties fought for supremacy (Stone 1990).[12] By the mid-to-late 1980s, dons were no longer so strongly politically motivated, as their activities had diversified. They now participated in racketeering schemes, drug trafficking overseas, legitimate businesses in construction, entertainment, and mining as well as extortion, robberies, and contract killings. In the post-1970s era, dons were able to deepen their embedded power in garrisons because they had more wealth and more high-powered weapons. Dons use these to influence residents to 'buy into' their spheres of power and control. At times, they employed fear and violence to reinforce their status as the "don of dons" or the "real ghetto governors".[13]

The Impact of Drugs on the Social Power of Dons

Political Polarisation and Dons: The mid-1960s into the 1970s were intense periods in Jamaica's political history. The two major political parties found work for the idle and often violent hands of Kingston's "lumpenproletariat".[14] The violence of the 1970s was more widespread than the 1960s, fuelled by battles between major political gangs. The ideological currents of the Cold War also influenced these posses and the dons that ran them. The PNP, a left-leaning party, was strongly influenced by socialist ideas during the 1970s. In fact, Prime Minister Michael Manley (PNP) was a close associate of Fidel Castro of Cuba. Manley's governments from 1972 to 1980 embraced a political model labelled Democratic Socialism. Under Manley, the Jamaican government engaged in community-based development and self-reliance programmes and sought to increase Jamaica's trade with Non-Aligned countries.[15] Manley's governments sought to base the nation's economy on state ownership of industries including the railway, power and water, agriculture, and mining. The JLP, a right-leaning party, formed Jamaica's government in 1980 under the leadership of Edward Seaga. The Party and its leader were pro-capitalist and supportive of the US/UK neoliberal policies of the 1980s. Seaga was a close ally of the Ronald Reagan administration and a prominent leader of the US-sponsored Caribbean Basin Initiative[16] in 1984.

During the 1970s, Jamaica became a high debt economy; its debt-to-GDP ratio since that decade has remained among the highest in the world. In 2011, the World Bank, in "Jamaica: Country Economic Memorandum: Unlocking Growth" concluded, "Jamaica was one of the world's slowest-growing economies in the last four decades. In the 2000s, Jamaica's average real GDP growth ranked 180th out of 196 countries. Jamaica's ranking in terms of average real GDP growth continuously deteriorated during 1960–2008."[17] The decade of the 1970s left in its wake well-armed dons who now lacked past sources of political and fiscal support. It also left behind urban communities polarised by a divisive political culture fed by violence and antagonistic social identities. The combination of violence and slow or negative economic growth led to deterioration in living conditions in the nation's garrisons in the 1980s. Meanwhile, and for the reasons just outlined, the state was economically constrained and unable to respond to the needs of Jamaica's urban poor. This socio-political and economic context provided the conditions for a new breed of dons and gangs to emerge. Figure 5.3 traces the impact of drug trafficking on the evolution of and the roles played by dons in Jamaica's garrison communities.

Figure 5.3: Impact of Drug and Gun Trafficking on Roles of Dons (1970s–2012)

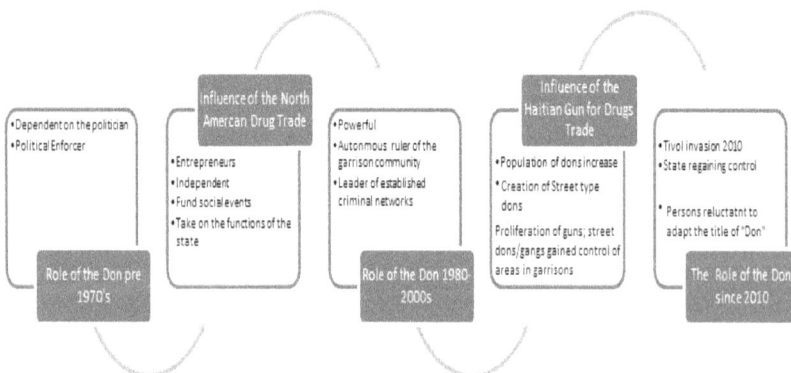

Cocaine and Marijuana: One of Jamaica's deputy commissioners of police who was once in charge of Jamaica's transnational and organised crime unit (Operation Kingfish)[18] discussed the shift dons made from financially depending on political clientelist associations in an interview with me.

> Jamaica was targeted as a transhipment point. With dons not getting what they were used to getting from the political process, they turned to drugs, so then these South Americans would come to Jamaica and form associations with local dons or vice versa. So the trade developed where loads of cocaine would come up out of Colombia and it would be secured by some of our local dons, and as payment, some of the dons were paid in small quantities of cocaine. (Interview, October 13, 2011: VT023)

Drug trafficking became a new and more lucrative source of funding for garrison dons. *The International Narcotics Control Strategy Report* has suggested that Jamaica remains the largest supplier of marijuana to the United States (2011, 325). In fact, Jamaica was a major supplier of marijuana to North American markets (USA/Canada) long before the 1980s (Campbell, 1987). Cocaine also was significant. Figure 5.4 shows the importance of the Caribbean region to cocaine trafficking into the US in the 1980s. By 1981, the Caribbean corridor was a significant supplier of cocaine to the US Drugs, transhipped through the region passed through the hands of local traffickers and dealers.

Cocaine trafficking from South America was a game changer for the local gangs and dons in Jamaica's garrisons in the 1980s. Dons and gangs struck 'white gold' in cocaine; they were able to set up drug-selling networks across the US and in the UK. With the transhipment of cocaine through Jamaican seaports and the "courier drug trade" via the airline industry (Air Jamaica, in particular) in the 1980s, criminal gangs and organised crime grew strongly, particularly in the West Kingston region. Beyond their own nation's shores, Jamaican dons and gangs developed operations on the streets of Brooklyn and the Bronx in New York, and Miami, Florida, shipping and selling cocaine and marijuana (Gunst 1996).

Figure 5.4: Drug Route through the Caribbean

**Cocaine introduced in the United States by corridor,
1981-2001**
(by percentage)

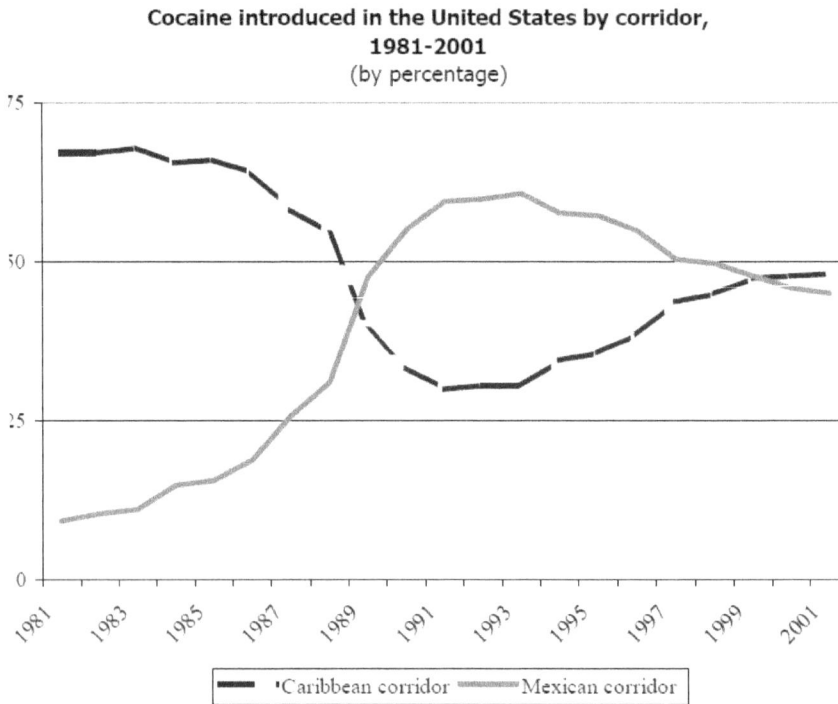

*Source: United Nations Office of Drugs and Crime (UNOC), 2003 Caribbean
Drug Trends (4) Retrieved from http://www.unodc.org/pdf/barbados/caribbean_
drug-trends_2001-2002.pdf*

Trafficking and selling drugs at home and especially abroad
financially empowered mega dons to provide social services to residents
of their home garrisons. They also used some of the proceeds of their
drug running to contribute money to the political parties aligned with
their garrisons. Additionally, they used their wealth to co-opt and 'pay-
off' (and thereby corrupt) police, military, and coast guard officials.
Gunst (1996) has detailed in her work, *Born fi Dead*, that a gang from
the Southeast St Andrew community of McGregor Gully in Jamaica
called the "Gulley men" led by a mega don, Eric "Chineyman" Vassell,
had a strong drug-selling network across the state of New York in the
1980s. Using proceeds from that operation, the Gully men sent barrels
of clothing and food, weapons, and money transfers to McGregor Gully.
Interviewee VT006, a resident of a garrison community and a senior

social worker in a state-funded inner-city intervention agency, argued that drugs in the 1980s-1990s played a significant role in creating a "new breed" of Jamaican dons. Dons, he stressed, were no longer partisan puppets; they participated in several local and international businesses (criminal and legitimate). After 1980, dons were:

> Involved in buying and selling of weapons, drug trade, and extortion, involved in major high-profile robberies. These dons have access to significant resources, their contacts and influence stretch overseas so they have access to significant resources, and they use the community as a vehicle to further the development of their own business empire and criminal network. (Interview September 1, 2011: VT006)

After the 1960s and 1970s, dons no longer had control over communities via political support and resources. Instead, as Amanda Sives said, "the flow of hard drugs through the Caribbean during the 1980s and 1990s combined with the tightening of state resources has provided another, more lucrative avenue for income generation" (2002, 84). The trafficking of marijuana and cocaine through the Caribbean into US and UK markets took place despite US efforts to wage a "war on drugs" as demand for these substances outpaced authorities' capacities to interdict their supply.

In 1971, US President Richard Nixon declared drugs to be "public enemy number one" (Baum, 1996). The US targeted "producer" states in South America[19] as the problem and directed funds and law enforcement to eradicate the drug "scourge" at the source. The real problem, however, especially in the 1980s, was increased demand for cocaine in the US. Americans during this period had a seemingly insatiable appetite for crack-cocaine, marijuana, and heroin (Marez 2004). According to data from the UNOC 2010 report, the US remains the "single largest national cocaine market" (72). The report notes that in 1981 an estimated 10.5 million people in the US used cocaine (72).[20] Along with the huge market for cocaine and marijuana, consumption in the US encouraged the rise of the Medellin cartel in Colombia. Drug-kingpins, Pablo Escobar, Carolos Lehder, Jose Gonzalo Rodriguez Gacha and the Ochoa family formed an alliance to manufacture and traffic cocaine into the United States.[21] VT023 (a deputy commissioner of police-DCP) suggested that local dons developed alliances with the

Colombians to tranship loads of cocaine into the United States. For the first time during this period, Jamaican elected officials began to view dons not as allies but as threats to their hegemony in garrison neighbourhoods. The DCP stated that scores of dons migrated during the 1980s to the US as the local economic and political climate changed. With the help of the police, party officials from the PNP and the JLP sought increasingly to prosecute or exterminate the dons with whom they had previously worked closely. Dons who migrated, according to Interviewee VT023,

> Were providing support to gangs, they were receiving the loads of cocaine; they were converting it, selling it and sending guns down or money down. So what it means they were also paving the way that if deported, then they have a family-a gang family to come back to. (Interview, October 13, 2011: VT023)

In a statement to the Southern New York US District Court, cooperating witness one (CW-1)[22] in the Christopher "Dudus" Coke case offered a vivid picture of the influence of drug trafficking on the power of dons from as early as the 1980s onwards. The witness testified that Dudus had network connections with Jamaicans who lived in and sold drugs in New York City and Miami. In exchange for the cocaine that Christopher Coke sent them, the mega don received guns. As CW-1 stated,

> Dudus said, in substance, that he needed to obtain more high-powered weapons because through having "heavy machines" such as rifles, he could have more power. I understood this to mean both power within the Organisation (the Shower Posse) but also within Jamaica". (Written Court Statement, May 21, 2012)

One interviewee from Brown Villa remarked, "The more guns a don has, the more powerful he is" (Interview October 25, 2011: VT027). The drug trade made Coke wealthy and very powerful inside the Jamaican criminal underworld. He was also an entrepreneur and developed legitimate businesses in construction and the retail industry (clothing and food). Coke exemplified the new breed of Jamaican don, embedded deeply inside his Tivoli Gardens garrison. Interviewee VT001 (journalist) in commenting on the influence of the drug trade on the changing nature of the power and roles of dons, remarked:

The turn of the 1970s and 80s, and the rise of the drug culture in Jamaica [was] where we shifted from the traditional ganja production and export to hard drugs; what you had emerging was a different kind of don. There are those early dons who did not have the business acumen of a Coke (Dudus). They simply commanded influence and authority through sheer violence, the will to perpetrate violence on behalf of the politician. He (dons) has evolved over time from being a mere political organiser/enforcer to one who is a major political and economic player (Interview, July 26, 2011).

Several other Brown Villa interviewees (nine CBO and clergy members in total) suggested that two major dons emerged in the community from the early 1990s into the 2000s because of their involvement in drug running (the same area dons X and Y mentioned above).

According to VT007 (an NGO/CBO director), one don in Brown Villa had strong control over a large segment of the community. He attributed that individual's power in Brown Villa to his involvement in drug trafficking and to his political connections that gave him major contracts to fix roads and collect garbage in the community. The don was also a record producer and a major investor in one of the community's football (soccer) teams and sports complexes. This don is an area don; he has strong business acumen, and he has long considered Brown Villa home. Several interviewees called him a "community don". That is, he was perceived as having made considerable contributions to the garrison's welfare and development.

The other area don who emerged in the 1990s (Don Y) used parts of Brown Villa as an outlet to sell cocaine. Interviewees saw him less as a "community don" and more as someone focused on his drug-running enterprise. Although he had political connections, this don focused more on selling and trafficking cocaine; he was also a music producer and had several retail businesses. This don also exemplified the new breed of dons: self-interested business persons who use the garrison communities in which they operate as outlets and administrative headquarters. Don Y was a powerful area don. However, what distinguished him from Don X was his relative lack of concern to "give back" to his community. In talking with interviewee VT028, the issue of personality differences among dons arose. She observed that dons have distinct individual personalities and that a garrison could have dons with similar financial power, but divergent approaches to community welfare, for example. Some dons tend to have more autocratic and violent means of exercising their authority, while others employ less punitive measures and styles of governing. According to VT028:

> My experience with the dons now is that they come with different degrees of 'wickedness' and they also come with different degrees of quote-end-quote progressiveness. There are the men that will support the community development programmes in the organisations that I have been a part of. And when you establish for example a school programme in the evenings, this kind of don will say to a 'would be shotta' (potential gangster) make sure you go to the school). At the bottom of the same street, you have a pathological, I mean real ill, sick, sick, sick type of don; beheads people, real sick, and then brags about it. (Interview, October 25. 2011: VT028)

Residents from another section of Brown Villa mentioned that the don for their area acquired control because of his wealth and 'fire power' (arsenal of weapons). In describing this individual, interviewee VT020 stated, "Don 'Z' grew up in the community and went away to Canada, he was into drug selling and when he came back to Jamaica, he bought his donmanship from another don for US$100,000" (Interview October 11, 2011: VT020). This information is difficult to verify. However, a senior superintendent of police (VT022) in the West Kingston police division mentioned that "Don Z" was wealthy from his drug running and that it was very likely that he exchanged cash for control of the Brown Villa district in which he operated. That district of Brown Villa has a strong partisan connection to the community and don where "Don Z" allegedly purchased his donmanship. This method of becoming a don in the post-1970s era supports the view that Jamaican dons are now enmeshed in complex economic and political enterprises and networks. They have become involved in activities that have further enriched them and are able to exercise force and distribute material resources among garrison residents. The evidence indicates that drug trafficking proceeds accelerated dons' rise to prominence in garrison neighbourhoods.

This new breed of dons has embedded itself in garrisons by using the community as centres for their economic operations (both criminal and legitimate). In these areas, they can buy the loyalty of residents; they get cheap labour from unemployed youth, and they serve as benefactors to residents to the degree it furthers their hegemonic position and/or personal predilection. Interviewee VT023 (the DCP) suggested that dons/gangs have managed to embed themselves in garrisons because of their ability to co-opt several groups, including the church, NGOs, politicians, and the police. In his view,

> Dons are so powerful that they are able to co-opt the churches and NGOs in the area. They also co-opt the media as well; just look at the entertainment industry and how DJs and street dances are sponsored and supported by gangs, dons. They work well with peace management initiative groups; they have co-opted the entire process. (Interview, October 13, 2011: VT023)

A gun and marijuana trade between Jamaica and Haiti developed in the early years of the 2000s. This was a significant finding; it provides one explanation for the emergence of several corner gangs and street dons across the Kingston and metro areas. The evidence suggests that street dons are active across the five districts of the Brown Villa community.

The Haitian Connection: The trade between Jamaica and Haiti fostered another shift in the characteristics of "donmanship" in Jamaica's garrisons. In 2008, then Assistant Commissioner of Police in Jamaica Glenmore Hinds stated, "The trade between Jamaica and Haiti is very significant. The firearms that come from Haiti are mainly handguns, revolvers, pistols, and a few shotguns" (BBC News October 25, 2008).[23] The increased availability of guns from Haiti meant that lower-ranked gangs/dons could arm themselves and provide security and protection services to different corners and streets inside the larger garrison space. Interviewee VT023, a senior police officer, described how the guns-for-drugs trade between Jamaica and Haiti started:

> It came about, but it also coincided with the de-stabilisation in Haiti, where the Haitian army was disbanded, and so the Haitian streets were awash with guns. This was in late 2002 into 2003. Because of the fishing route between Jamaica and Haiti, our fishermen run to Haiti, and a few of them discovered that in Haiti the demand for good quality ganja was very high, and Haiti was

a major transhipment point for drugs going to the Bahamas and then the United States. The fishermen now sold the ganja to the Haitians, who paid them with guns. So when the fishermen came back they had to sell the guns because they had no real use for them. (Interview, October 13, 2011: VT023)

Street gangs and street dons evidently emerged out of the desire of some lower-status gang members ('shottas' or 'foot soldiers') to challenge the power and hegemonic positions of community-wide dons. In consequence, the post-1990s era has seen a decline in the domination of single dons over entire garrison communities. Coke was among the last cohort of dons to have complete control over an entire garrison space. Figure 5.5 highlights the impact that the gun-for-drugs trade has had on the availability of illegal guns, and the changes it has created in the features of don hierarchy and control in Jamaica's garrisons.

Figure 5.5: Impact of the Gun-for-Drugs-Trade between Jamaica and Haiti

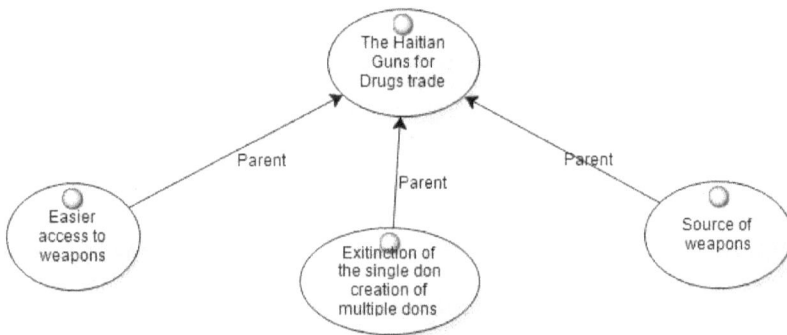

The Brown Villa case illustrates the broader shift that has taken place in the power structure of dons and gangs in Jamaica's garrisons. The community has had several street-level dons since the 2000s and two area dons from the 1990s onwards. Interviewee VT005 (a journalist), when commenting on the impact of the trade between Jamaica and Haiti on the don structure in garrisons, averred:

Christopher [Coke] is the last of Jamaica's great (mega) dons that have controlled a wide area, community with economic and military might. The access to cash by smaller people has led to this. The access to guns also contributes to this as well. … The drugs for guns from Haiti opened access to guns to communities. This access to guns and ammunition means that no one is now waiting on one single man or politician to get a gun; they can get their own guns. (Interview, August 11, 2011: VT005)

Similarly, interviewee VT023 argued that the guns-for-drugs trade had contributed significantly to the spread of guns and gun-related crimes to the rural parishes of Jamaica since 2005. Prior to 2005 up to "70 to 80 per cent of our gun-related crimes" were committed in the KMA in the parishes of Kingston, St Andrew, and St Catherine. VT023 noted that in the rural parishes of the island, wherever there are fishing villages, fishermen depart from those areas to go to Haiti and "exchange ganja for guns" (Interview October 13, 2011: VT023). In rural parishes such as Clarendon in south central and St James in western Jamaica, the senior police officer claimed that since "2006 there have been an increase in gun-related crimes – shooting, robberies and murder". One retired senior superintendent of police (JCF) pointed out in an interview with me that local garrison dons from Kingston and St Andrew travel to rural farming and fishing districts in Jamaica to engage in drug and gun smuggling (Interview, 19 Dec. 2011: VT041).

On an unrelated visit to a fishing village, a local fisherman described how guns and drugs are trafficked through the borders of Jamaica via the Caribbean Sea. The angler ("Yellow") shared that at night fishermen take loads of compressed marijuana to the Pedro Cays[24] and from there they make their way using fishing boats to Haiti. According to Yellow, the Pedro Cays sometimes serve as a holding area where anglers exchange marijuana for money with other fisher folk who make the journey to Haiti. Guns, especially handguns and sometimes rifles, are taken back to Jamaica. When asked about the risks involved in trafficking guns and marijuana, he responded that the greatest risks come from other anglers whom he called "pirates". One risk having their "boat load of food, weed or guns robbed by these vicious pirates".[24] Yellow also stated that sailors from the Jamaican Coast Guard sometimes receive cash to allow the free passage of guns and drugs. Regarding cocaine, Yellow noted that the "Colombians have some very fast boats, and they pay big money to fishermen to take cocaine to drop points near the Bahamas, Cuba and even Haiti".[26] Yellow's information is consistent with that which a police officer provided in an interview (VT023): "Haiti is a major transhipment point for drugs going to the Bahamas and then the United States" (Interview October 13, 2011: VT023). According to the *International Narcotics Control Strategy Report* (INSCR) of March 2012, "Haiti remains a transit point for cocaine originating in South America for transhipment to the United States, Canada, Europe, and elsewhere in the Caribbean" (INSCR, March 2012).[27] The Report also suggested that marijuana originating from Jamaica is a "concern" of the US and other hemispheric authorities.[28] The guns that Yellow said enter Jamaica via fishing villages end up in the hands of gangs and dons. Yellow remarked that sometimes anglers sell the guns to "powerful men". He refused to say what he meant by "powerful men", but indicated that buyers came from different parts of the metropolitan area (Kingston, St Catherine and St Andrew).

Evidence on the number of guns that have entered Jamaica via the 'Haitian corridor' is inconclusive. However, officials from the Transnational Crime and Narcotics Division and Operation Kingfish units of the JCF maintain that since the early 2000s significant amounts of guns and ammunition have entered Jamaica via Haiti (*Gleaner* June 14, 2011).[29] The main source of illegal guns and ammunition in Jamaica, however, continues to be ship containers carrying food, appliances, and motor vehicles. The JCF reports that very substantial shipments of illegal guns to Jamaica originate from the United States. In his sworn statement to the US District Court, CW-1 described how Coke trafficked guns into Jamaica in exchange for cocaine:

> Dudus explained that firearms sent from the United States are packaged in appliances, refrigerators, deep freezes, and that handguns and ammunition could also be sent down in foodstuffs, including rice and flour, as well as in soap boxes. I have seen the 'shotters' and high-level members of the Shower Posse, in Dudus' presence, dismantling these appliances and taking apart the foodstuffs to retrieve the firearms.[30] (Written Court Statement, May 21, 2012)

Gangs and dons use various means of acquiring wealth, weapons, and control over geographic turf inside garrisons and the business districts of town centres like Kingston. A senior police officer in narcotics asserted that "gangs must be resourced, and narcotics are one of the main ways of getting money and funds…They will depend on narcotics to maintain their lifestyle and power" (Interview November 7, 2011: VT031). The proceeds from drug selling and trafficking facilitated the creation of new types of dons in Jamaica. The money and guns gave them the capacity to play several roles inside garrisons. They are the ghetto "governors" in neighbourhoods where the state's power is anaemic and its elected officials devoid of political will to serve their constituents.

This chapter outlined the main roles dons have performed over the last several decades and how their activities have allowed them to establish often favourable political, socio-cultural and economic relationships with garrison residents. Contributing to the social welfare of residents and providing protection to their community members' lives and property are key governing roles that dons (predominantly mega and to a lesser extent area dons) have performed. It is not surprising that garrison residents, including those from Brown Villa, perceive dons as ghetto governors. The evidence also suggests that apart from supporting these leaders out of a sense of gratitude, garrison residents also support dons out of fear. Residents consent to the inherently violent hegemony of their dons as a deliberate strategy to secure their survival. They evidently consider the violence of jungle justice measures to be legitimate because of its swiftness and responsiveness to their pleas for justice.

Nonetheless, as Figure 5.2 indicates, May 2010 likely constituted a watershed moment in the control that dons have in garrison communities. The capture and extradition of one of Jamaica's last remaining mega dons, Christopher Coke, exposed the deeply embedded status that these men have nurtured since the late 1960s in Jamaica's garrisons. But it also signalled the demise of this type of community leader. Recent evidence indicates that the title of "don" is increasingly unpopular. Towards the end of all interviews I conducted, interviewees pointed out that dons were shunning such labels, and in fact, many were making themselves less visible inside their garrisons.

Sharply increased police patrols in inner-city communities and the targeting of dons and gangs after May 2010 allowed the state to embark on a process of reasserting its authority in Jamaica's garrisons. However, whatever the ultimate outcome of these national efforts to remove and/or supersede the dons may prove to be, the conditions that facilitated their emergence and evolution remain. Garrison communities such as Brown Villa suffer from poor infrastructural development, high rates of unemployment and ineffectual political representation. The Jamaican state remains weak in providing essential governance services to garrisons, and new types of dons have stepped in to fill the vacuum, even as the nation seeks to remove them. If it is to succeed, the Jamaican state through its law enforcement and social services branches of government must reposition itself as an active player in governing garrison communities. As this case study shows, today's Jamaican dons are criminal non-state actors whose roles have evolved with the shifting tides of the global political economy as well as that in the neighbourhoods in which they are active. Their influence on Jamaica's governments and local communities requires more attention in the literature on governance in the Caribbean.

SIX

Disempowering Dons

Introduction

Dons have performed security and social welfare functions in Jamaica's garrison communities at different times in recent decades. These individuals tend to carry out roles associated with the provision of social welfare, security/protection, political partisan mobilisation and the maintenance of law, order and control using "jungle justice" measures. They have been able to embed themselves in garrison neighbourhoods, which are usually steeped in poverty and prone to violence, by gaining the trust and support of residents, who often perceive dons as protectors and providers. Dons' performance of such roles allows them to serve as embedded governing authorities in garrison communities. The findings from a close study of Brown Villa concerning the roles of violent non-state actors suggest it may be appropriate to re-think the nature of governance and the actors we view as legitimate holders of power and authority.

Examples of the power of the Sicilian Mafia and Jamaican dons shed light on the influence that violent groups and individuals have in contexts where the state's capacity to govern is weak or weakening. Aside from the issue of fragile state capacity, political corruption provides a fertile environment for such actors to play influential roles within and across the borders of the state. Some Jamaican dons, for example, have been involved in local and global economic markets (both legal and illegal) and in some communities, they have served as active players in delivering public services, such as garbage disposal and transportation. This research suggests that the academic community, particularly Caribbean scholars, and policymakers, would do well to explore critically what lessons can be learned about the state and governance by focusing attention on the actions of criminal entities. At least some states do not possess a monopoly over popularly legitimated authority. The roles dons have developed in Brown Villa provide strong illustrations of that reality.

The violence and criminality associated with dons and their gangs are not uniform across Jamaica. The epicentres of drug, gang and politically charged violence are in the urban inner-city communities in the parishes of Kingston, St Andrew, and St Catherine. Likewise, not all of Jamaica's inner cities are garrison communities. Dons and garrisons alike first emerged because of deliberate attempts by the Jamaica Labour Party (JLP) and the People's National Party (PNP) to secure support and electoral victories. Both phenomena (garrisons and their informal leaders) should be carefully analysed in context to safeguard against over-generalisations.

In May 2010, the Jamaican government used military and police units to enter Tivoli Gardens to arrest and extradite drug lord and garrison don Christopher "Dudus" Coke to the United States. Tivoli residents staged a large public protest in response to the state's action. Female garrison residents marched in white T-shirts around the community crying for "justice", and many neighbourhood men erected barricades at the major entrances to the community. One female resident had a placard that read, "Jesus died for us, we will die for Dudus." This statement became a national headline. Indeed, many Jamaicans who live outside the confines of garrison communities were outraged at the blatant disregard shown towards the state, law, and order. The impasse between the security forces and criminal gangs loyal to Coke sparked interest in understanding better the reasons that might underpin such a public display of support for a drug lord and garrison don. Who was Coke, really? And what kinds of things do the dons do inside garrison communities to earn such standing and popular support? Were dons, in fact, predators who employ fear to exercise autocratic rule over garrison residents? The popular support for Coke also raised the question of whether dons might indeed enjoy the voluntary backing and loyalty of garrison residents, and if so, why? Linked to these questions, is the lingering assessment of what factors might account for the emergence and then the gradual transformation of dons over time from serving as enforcers for political parties in Jamaica (1960s/1970s) to their most recent role as violent entrepreneurs[1] (late 1980s onwards). The national government's Tivoli incursion gave rise to a questioning of the legitimacy and power of the Jamaican state inside garrison areas.

Embedded Governance

Dons are embedded governance actors inside Jamaica's garrison communities. This is one explanation for the popular support some dons receive from garrison residents. Despite their despotic style of rule and frequent use of violent force, dons have been given titles such as "community godfathers", "ghetto governors" or "chief welfare officers".[2] Viewing dons as embedded governing actors allows a reassessment of the pillars upon which legitimate authority and control rest. That is, the source, character, and foundations of legitimate authority. Does it derive from the masses or a smaller group, such as the economic and political elite? The Brown Villa case suggests that the community roots of legitimacy and authority are tied to residents' calculated assent or disapproval of governing actors which includes dons.

A don becomes embedded within a community given the length of time he is associated with a garrison; the frequency with which he distributes material resources within that garrison; his provision of security and protection to residents, his involvement in entertainment, infrastructural development and social projects within the community, foster embeddedness. As this process unfolds, garrison residents learn to rely on and invest their trust in community dons to help to secure their economic survival and personal safety. This reliance developed in the face of the absence or evanescence of the state's authority in garrison communities.

On one level, the garrison environment itself may be said to facilitate the embedding of dons and gangs. The conditions of high unemployment, more than 65 per cent in Brown Villa in 2011 (SDC[3] 2011), insecurity from frequent gang-related rivalries and poor educational attainment among the youth, allow dons to acquire and maintain high social rank and legitimacy among residents. Chapter four contends that the social, economic, and political setting of Brown Villa made it possible for a series of different types of dons (area and street dons particularly) to emerge and establish relational ties with residents. Each district of Brown Villa has its own street don, and the northern section of the community still has an area don (Don Y mentioned in chapter five). In most cases, residents see the don more than they see their elected representatives. If there is a problem with sewage or garbage pollution, for example, the don sometimes directs his local trucking company to clean the debris from the streets of the community, while the public authority remains distant and at least apparently unresponsive.

Brown Villa, like other garrison communities in Jamaica, is comprised of lower-income households with limited access to education and training. Given the low human capital (skills and training) among residents, especially the young (ages 14–25), dons/gangs can recruit fresh members. Dons, especially mega and area types, have come to symbolise wealth and power; this attracts the younger as well as other older residents. Women find some dons attractive because of the symbolic riches, prestige and authority associated with "donmanship". In some cases, recruitment is not required. As one interviewee, a former member of a gang (VT021) in the 1970s and now a leader of a CBO in Brown Villa, pointed out to me, many youths in the community do not wait to be approached; they often volunteer to join the dons' "system". Many of these young people (generally men) find it difficult and apparently less alluring to enter the official structures of the Jamaican economy. Additionally, many young men, often lacking clear alternative role models in their communities, see dons and gang leaders as masculine prototypes, as supposed "real men" whom they wish to emulate.[4] Jamaican garrisons, like other urban inner-city communities in other nations in the Caribbean and Latin America, including Guatemala, Nicaragua, and Venezuela, are characterised by socio-economic conditions that encourage the embedding of rogue actors.

If political and economic settings are initially conducive, the roles dons perform surely facilitate their social embedding within garrisons. This process takes place at the individual, household/family and communal levels. The failure of successive governments to alleviate grinding conditions of poverty, both private and public, in places such as Brown Villa has resulted in the loss of residents' confidence in the capacity of the state to undertake efforts to help to improve their living conditions. Since the late 1970s, the Jamaican state has failed to assert and maintain its version of law and order in garrisons. The state has in effect lost its centralised authority and legitimacy within many poor inner-city communities. Dons have stepped into that vacuum and filled the social welfare gaps left by the invisible or retreating (neoliberal) state. Garrison residents, as those in Brown Villa exemplify, have often been reluctant to collaborate and engage in dialogue with representatives of the Jamaican government, especially the police. An important capacity that the state is expected to possess is the ability to provide security to its citizens. As the work of Peter Evans et al. (1985) has suggested, the state needs to reassert its role in the governance process. This rings true in the Jamaican context if the primary reasons for the rise of the legitimacy of dons are to be overcome.

Dons demonstrate their governing capacity best in the crucial area of community security and protection. Residents, clergy officials and approximately 65 per cent of CBO interviewees noted that in times of inter-gang warfare, the police often have not been present, and the don and his gang have ensured the community's security. Nonetheless, the equation is hardly one-sided. The don and his gang members have systematically used organised violence and force to embed themselves in their communities. As a result, violence, social instability, and a crippling culture of fear usually exist simultaneously among garrison residents. As suggested in chapter five, dissenters to the don's authority and system of control receive severe punishment.

Nonetheless, violent actors or not, dons also appear to develop affective or social bonds with the residents of the garrisons in which they operate. The examples of dons such as Eric Vassell from McGregor Gully, Christopher Coke from Tivoli Gardens and Don "X" from Brown Villa, illustrate the socio-cultural influence and ties to their communities such informal leaders may develop. Sponsorship of Easter and Christmas gatherings and providing gifts to children and adults, especially at Christmas, are culturally symbolic and significant efforts that these dons have undertaken and that have endeared them to garrison residents. Easter and Christmas festivities date to the era of plantation slavery in Jamaica and the rest of the Anglo-Caribbean. Dons' hosting of community reggae concerts and dancehall street shows inside garrison communities offers residents opportunities to earn sporadic income by selling their wares (cigarettes, gum, and marijuana) or serving as bartenders (women) or informal security (men). These musical events are important features of Jamaican popular culture, and they resonate with garrison residents.

Don Typology

The altercation between criminal thugs loyal to Christopher Coke and Jamaica's security forces was impressive. Coke was able to marshal the support and respect of many of his community's residents, even as he and his supporters had amassed sufficient weaponry to confront the state's police and military units. Also striking were the 1998 street protests launched by residents loyal to Matthews Lane's don Donald "Zekes" Phipps,[5] who was arrested by police on criminal charges. That neighbourhood's residents demanded that the state release "their" don as he provided for them and ensured their safety. The expectation that the don role everywhere was the same and that all such individuals were wealthy, involved in drug trafficking and offered social services to their garrisons that Jamaican governments were unable or otherwise unwilling to deliver was dispelled.

The examination of the phenomenon of Jamaica's dons revealed that they took on a range of roles at different levels and with different areas of influence, giving rise to a necessity to categorise them into different types: mega, area and street. Placing dons into different categories may have analytical value as it provides a strategic frame for the study of similar criminal groups and violent actors in the wider Latin America and Caribbean region. Not all leaders and groups operating illegally (in this case dons and their gangs) are the same. Contextual analysis is important to identify disparities in organisational structures, ideologies, and the variety of activities they perform. Thinking of non-state criminal actors such as dons as reflecting various types can assist scholars in the fields of comparative politics and criminology by sensitising them to the possible differences in authority and governance activities that these leaders manifest.

The mega don was the most powerful don type. These individuals tend to have strong criminal and financial network connections, both locally and internationally. According to those interviewed, Brown Villa does not currently have such an individual in its midst. Indeed, the garrison's last mega don was killed in the early 1980s during the intense gun battles between JLP- and PNP-endorsed thugs. Christopher "Dudus" Coke (1990s–2010), his father Lester Lloyd "Jim Brown" Coke (1980s–1990s) and Donald "Zekes" Phipps (1990s) are the most recent examples of mega dons to operate and control territory in the Kingston metropolitan area. Mega dons exhibit strong business acumen and depend on narcotics and gun trafficking as their main sources of wealth. They also engage in legitimate businesses in the construction, transportation, entertainment, and sports industries. The mega don fits the definition of a "violent entrepreneur". These dons, like their area counterparts, are willing to take risks to develop commercial and trade prospects. This area of initiative opened for them as they transitioned from being partisan enforcers for the JLP/PNP to becoming strong and independent business and political leaders of their communities.

Area dons tend to have fewer material resources at their disposal than mega dons can command, and they do not have inter-community (and beyond) reach, as mega dons do. Police, NGO officials, journalists and residents indicated that Brown Villa had two area dons, and these had been in place since the 1990s. And, as earlier noted, one of those is now dead. Area dons generally control single communities or neighbourhoods within them, and they often work as surrogates for mega dons as they conduct their licit and illicit business affairs. Both types have the resources and strong community support among residents to perform social welfare roles, such as paying school tuition fees for children or distributing household supplies to neighbourhood residents. Additionally, they have ties with the major political parties in Jamaica. The Brown Villa case suggested that both mega and area dons still rely on elected representatives to provide them with government contracts and political "cover" to legitimate their presence in garrisons. Political parties in Jamaica first gave rise to the dons, and even today, the umbilical cord between elected officials and dons remains intact.

There is no active mega don in Kingston at present; Coke seems to have been the last of this don type, at least for the moment. However, more dons of Coke's reach and stature will emerge if the socio-economic conditions of garrisons (discussed in chapter four) remain and elected officials continue to give succour to such actors for partisan ends. Criminal actors will take advantage of the opportunities that the global trafficking of illicit goods offers. The Caribbean region is still an active corridor through which contraband such as cocaine, illegal cigarettes and marijuana are transhipped. If these conditions remain unchanged, future mega dons appear likely.

The street don is a recent development, dating only to the late 1990s or early years of the present century. These dons, unlike their mega and area counterparts, lack the financial resources to perform social welfare as an ongoing role. In fact, in some cases, they are known to have extorted resources from community residents. This category of dons appears to be the most volatile sort. They usually are less committed to their community's development and much more involved in intra-garrison gang battles to secure or maintain control over turf. Street dons assume responsibility for the security of the turf they control. Residents of Brown Villa largely viewed them as a necessary evil, particularly during periods of intensive intra-and inter-gang feuds. Street dons tend to be younger, have limited partisan loyalties and often exhibit interest in challenging the control of their more powerful area don counterparts for leadership. In general, one becomes a mega or area don if one has the following "qualifications". He:

- Can develop and maintain widespread influence and appeal with community residents (Christopher Coke had such a connection).
- Possesses the capacity to instil fear and deference among residents, usually through jungle justice measures.
- Enjoys a monopoly over access to political spoils in the form of government contracts (construction/road maintenance/drain cleaning).
- Has complete control (in the case of mega dons) over the access and distribution of weapons and ammunition inside home garrisons and across other neighbourhoods as well. For their part,

area dons are usually shareholders in the access/distribution of weapons, and they tend to work within a specified territory.

- Can ensure a constant influx of cash from various sources such as the narcotics trade, extortion rackets, and illicit contraband trade (cigarettes). The don may also glean such resources from overseas remittances from satellite groups/individuals, usually from the US and the UK.

- Demonstrates willingness (present and past) to kill rival gang members/dons and to use extreme force on individuals and families who have not obeyed his orders or honoured his status in the community.

- Can exert influence across geographic jurisdictions if he is a mega don; that is, in satellite communities outside his home garrison. Area dons, on the other hand, tend to control a single community, while street dons exercise influence over avenues inside a single garrison.

To become a street don, one must exhibit (using the exact observations shared by several former street gang members):

- Access to guns (at least three guns are typically necessary to control a particular corner/avenue).

- Possession of cash, usually obtained from overseas contacts, to lure others to join gangs. Be able to get cash from robberies of transportation networks (bus/taxis) that run across the city of Kingston and adjoining areas.

- Show the willingness (and evidence of having done so in the past) to murder rivals and the capacity to instil fear among residents.

Based on the roles dons (mega, area and street) perform and the relationships they have forged with their communities, residents and people who work inside garrisons have formed impressions of who they really are. Figure 6.1 shows the interviewees' perceptions of all types of dons. Table 6.1 and Figure 5.1 summarises the major roles different dons play in garrisons.

Figure 6.1: Interviewees' Perceptions of Dons' Status in Garrisons

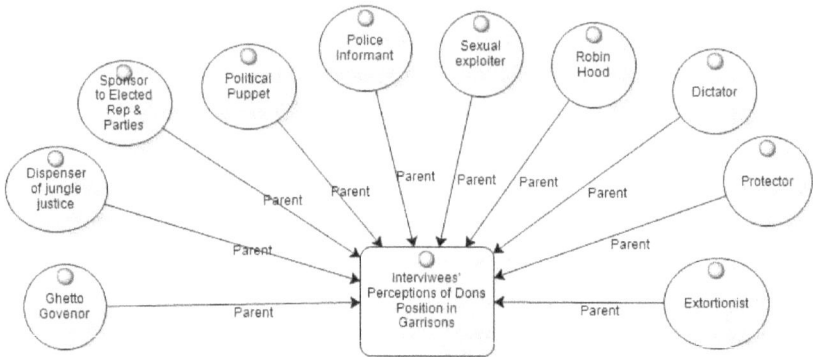

Table 6.1: Major Roles of Dons by Types

Don Type	Roles	Geographic Jurisdiction
Mega Dons	• Welfare/Security/Partisan Mobilization/Law, Order and Control via Jungle Justice	• Cross-Garrison/Parish
Area Dons	• Welfare/Security/Partisan Mobilization/Law, Order &Control	• Single-Garrison
Street Dons	• Security/Law, Order & Control via Jungle Justice	• Avenues within a single garrison

There is no uniformity to the phenomenon of garrisons. Brown Villa had six street dons, two area dons and a fragmented community structure. That division resulted from the influence of a polarised partisan culture/ identity and the authority and claims of its dons. In contrast, Tivoli Gardens, for example (not a part of this study), was centrally organised and administered by Christopher Coke and his father before him. That community has had a tradition of a single mega don and a uniform political alliance with the JLP. Some Brown Villa residents meanwhile demonstrate political allegiance to the PNP while others are aligned with the JLP. For analytic convenience, these community forms have been labelled as central authoritative and fragmented authoritative. There is a need and scope for further comparative research on the evolution and characteristics of these two garrison types in Jamaica.

Both of Jamaica's political parties deliberately developed opportunities for these leaders to emerge in the 1960s and 1970s to help mobilise their political supporters. Garrison residents are "underserved" and often neglected by their elected officials. This has been the case for several decades and the Brown Villa example illustrates the governance voids that exist in such neighbourhoods. In general, gangs operating in the nation's garrisons are prone to inter- and intra-gang rivalries over turf. These communities also evidence high rates of domestic violence, rates of homicide, limited economic opportunities and inadequate infrastructure maintenance and development (dilapidated buildings, roads, and broken sewer systems). Brown Villa is an example of a fragmented authoritative Jamaican garrison.

Drugs and Guns

Four central factors gave rise to Jamaica's dons. These are a deeply polarised partisan political culture; economic instability exacerbated by a neoliberal shift in state policy from the late 1970s onwards; the hollowing out of the state by neoliberal reforms (structural adjustment programmes) that opened space for dons; and the introduction, rapid growth and wild profitability of cocaine and gun trafficking. The Colombian cocaine trade from the 1980s onwards created a transnational market that connected South America, the Caribbean corridor, and North America. A new breed of dons emerged during the 1980s as this illegal commerce grew. The cocaine trade gave these criminal leaders greater financial resources and paramilitary capabilities. They used those resources (money and guns) to cement their control in garrison communities across the Kingston Metropolitan Area (KMA). A don such as Eric "Chineyman" Vassell, for example, was able to send barrels of clothing and household appliances to residents of his garrison community because of the drug-selling empire he operated in New York City.[6] Without the wealth from drug running and absent the weapons these dons were able to purchase, most of these leaders would not have had the ability to perform governing roles and, in so doing, acquire authority in places such as Brown Villa.

The Caribbean corridor during the 1980s and 1990s was a central supplier of cocaine to the United States. The Mexican-US border is now the main trade route for cocaine entering the US market. Drugs and guns are still trafficked, however, through the Caribbean with disastrous effects at the individual and community levels. Jamaica remains one node in the larger narcotics trade across the Americas. Consequently, the island experiences negative effects from its role in the narcotics trade. It has provided wealth and other resources to criminal groups such as dons and enables them to co-opt and buy out residents and pay off corrupt law enforcement officials. Political corruption in Jamaica and several countries across the region continue, literally, to be fed by the proceeds of drug trafficking.[7]

The guns-for-drugs trade between Jamaica and Haiti has had a direct impact on the types of dons active in garrisons. The street don emerged and multiplied in the 2000s in large part because of the access street gangs and corner crews[8] had to cheap weapons. Some of these guns, small pistols and revolvers enter Jamaica illegally via fishermen who traffic marijuana from Haiti. The trade between the two Caribbean states exemplifies the transnational nature of organised crime and the ingenuity of weapons and drug dealers. Guns and drugs move with ease across the porous national borders of the Caribbean. The relatively weak capacities of governments in these states to protect their borders and minimise corruption among customs officers, the coast guard and other law enforcement agency officials permit, even if it does not encourage, gun and drug trafficking.

The Haitian-Jamaican guns-for-drugs trade is a relatively new development that warrants further research. It appears at present, at least in part, that the flow of drugs through the region is shifting – moving laterally as opposed to vertically from the south to the north. In 2019, a senior member of the Jamaica Constabulary Force (JCF) remarked that the Jamaican-Haitian connection is expanding to include a "food-for-guns" variant. In this emerging episode of the contraband trade between the two nation-states, Haitian fisherfolk exchange weapons with their Jamaican counterparts for food items such as agricultural produce and meat. A high premium is placed on animal meats such as goats, cows, and chickens by illicit Haitian peddlers. The crisis of praedial larceny that afflicts Jamaica is now connected to the emergent food-for-drugs trade as local farmers suffer extensive losses, especially from farm-raised animals such as goats.[9]

Dissolving the Power of the Don

Dis-embedding dons from Jamaican garrisons such as Brown Villa will require collaboration among state officials, international and local non-governmental organisations, community-based associations (church/youth groups), the business sector and residents, who after all, are the central stakeholders. Added to this collaborative effort is the need for the state to re-assert its authority. This means increasing police patrols and setting up command posts and checkpoints at strategic locations inside identified garrison communities. Dismantling the power of dons will require strategies of sociological, economic, infrastructural, and political reform.

States of Emergency: In response to the escalation of violent crimes and gang activity, the Government of Jamaica (GOJ) put together legislation to ensure citizen security and strengthen its control in geographic areas with high levels of gang-related crimes and violence. The new crime initiative (Law Reform Act)[10] gave the GOJ emergency powers to detain and deport suspicious persons, enter premises and seize property without a warrant, and declare curfews. In January 2018, the GOJ declared States of Emergency (SOE) and Zones of Special Operations (ZOSOs) for several parishes including the Kingston Metropolitan Area (KMA) and the parish of St James. Since then, the GOJ has used SOEs and ZOZOs as security tools to go after organised crime bosses and gangs, and to bring social order and safety to communities inundated with violence.

Several garrison neighbourhoods between 2018 and 2021 have undergone periods of extended curfews and the establishment of security checkpoints by joint military and police personnel. While this strategy has led to marked levels of decline in crime and violence in these communities, the impact is temporary. When SOEs are lifted in these troubled geographic zones, high rates of gang-related shootings, homicides and crime steadily return. The status and operation of dons and gangs is disrupted by this strategy; however, it would require the GOJ to establish a permanent para-military base in garrison communities to achieve long-term improvements. Such a move is neither feasible in logistical terms nor is it beneficial to civic engagement and the cultivation of democratic values among residents in garrison neighbourhoods. SOEs and ZOZOs suspend several rights (for example, freedom of movement and assembly) citizens in these spaces have. As a short-term measure of disruption and containment of dons and gangs, states of emergencies and zones of special operations are useful and effective tools. However, a more sustainable and longer-term approach requires a shift in how policing is done in Jamaica's inner cities and violence-prone communities.

Reformed policing: Several community policing initiatives were being implemented in Brown Villa during the research. However, residents noted their reluctance to collaborate fully with and trust the police. The Jamaican state needs to dedicate more human and capital resources to policing efforts that treat individuals in garrison communities as citizens who are respected and their rights promoted and protected. The community residents interviewed complained that the community-policing unit in Brown Villa was not visible and active. It is important that social capital and trust are built between the police and residents, as it facilitates a stronger communicative and reciprocal relationship. Residents will be more willing to engage with the police in their communities and thereby less reluctant to cower behind the walls of silence out of fear of reprisal attacks from gangs and dons. Police officers attached to community-policing units require more training on how to enter social partnerships with residents to help with identifying violence producers.

Rehabilitation Services: Garrison spaces in Jamaica are war-torn areas; their residents have experienced intense gang/don and/or political violence over a sustained period. As interviews were conducted with residents in Brown Villa, it became apparent that there is a need for "grieving" and an avenue to process the trauma associated with living in garrisons beleaguered by violence. As one respondent pointed out, "we just bury the dead and go to funerals, but there is no grieving" (Interview, VT035). Mothers who have lost sons to gang-related violence and young men who witness their fathers murdered. These post-traumatic experiences encourage attitudes of resentment, hatred, and reprisal attacks.

Counselling for residents on a sustained basis is an important measure to help with the process of healing and repair in garrison neighbourhoods. Often, a don's social power and status inside garrisons is bolstered by the reliance some residents place on them to serve as agents of dispute resolution and access to social justice (often in the form of "jungle justice"). The practices of "jungle justice" can be replaced with authentic community-based restorative rehabilitative practices, values, and services. To facilitate this process of restoration, community councils can be formed. Community councils should include non-governmental and community-based groups, the police, elected officials, former gang members and residents. The Peace Management Initiative (PMI) group is a critical player in forging talks with rival gangs, dons and residents in Brown Villa and other neighbouring garrisons. The GOJ and other security stakeholders should listen to the experiences and advice of non-governmental organisations such as the PMI and collaborate with them.

Economic and Business Opportunities: The Jamaican state has failed to provide a stable social environment conducive to growth and development, particularly inside garrison neighbourhoods. If the challenges of low economic growth, social inequality and fragile state control in these spaces are not addressed, then the power and authority status the dons and gangs enjoy will remain firmly entrenched. Former gang members and residents note that some dons have the capacity to provide jobs and distribute financial support to people in need. In a context where there is an absence of government or private sector economic opportunities, the status and power of dons as economic benefactors increase and expand. As one respondent remarked, "as long as a man is hungry and dependent, he will forever support garrison politics and donmanship" (Interview, 2011: VT032). Brown Villa has no factories or commercial buildings. The private and corporate sectors should be central actors in this initiative of establishing business offices in these communities. The market must be visible inside garrisons which can have an economic and psychological impact on residents. Those interviewees who live in Brown Villa pointed out that they feel isolated from the business world and formal economy in Jamaica. If the GOJ can provide economic opportunities and infrastructural re-development in garrisons, the socio-economic prowess that some dons (especially the area and mega don types) have in garrisons can be dissolved.

Political Reform: The rise of dons and gangs in Jamaica have its early origins with the nation's political independence. In an ironic twist, the two major political parties after the nation's independence in 1962, vied for political power through the democratic processes of voting and party-based representation. This political competition, however, was intense, adversarial, and violent. Dons and gangs were used as political tools to enforce party loyalties and to mobilise support among the urban masses in Jamaican cities and towns across the island. The political battles and violence were pronounced in the parishes of Kingston, St Andrew, and adjoining metro areas. Political representatives and elected officials must initiate and sustain a moral, ethical, and legislative process of disassociating themselves and their political parties from organised criminal syndicates and the dons that lead them. It is not enough for elected representatives to sign political codes of conduct and make verbal commitments to act in moral and ethical ways while in office. Going a step further, the establishment of oversight auditing committees with prosecutorial powers may be useful in serving as a check and balance mechanism on the administrative functions of Members of Parliament (MPs) and Councillors in their respective constituencies. The ties that some elected officials have long held with gangs and dons must be broken. Elected officials who breach the political code of conduct by engaging in cronyism and corrupt transactions with garrison dons and gangs should face criminal investigations and prosecution.

Jamaica at its independence adopted and then adapted the British Westminster Parliamentary model of democratic government. One area that requires urgent reform is the majoritarian first-past-the-post electoral formula (FPTP). This approach embraces a 'winner-takes-all' outcome for general elections for the winning political party. As presented in chapters four and five, elected officials have depended on dons and their thugs to secure electoral victory by ensuring the relevant party receives the necessary votes to win. The current electoral formula FPTP encourages the polarised and adversarial partisan political culture that obtains in Jamaica. Elected officials should revisit the policies and laws of electoral administration in Jamaica. A shift from the FPTP formula may serve to ease the intensely competitive nature of electoral politics and thereby reduce the relevance of dons in the democratic process of voting.

Disrupting Transnational Links: Gangs and dons benefit from the proceeds of global transnational connections with Jamaicans residing in the US, the UK and Canada. Through these transnational networked relationships, handguns, small arms, ammunition, and cash are sent to Jamaican dons to ensure that they (dons) maintain their social power and para-military prowess in communities across the island. As one former gang member told me in an interview, dons use their transnational links to "lock" their turf, pay foot soldiers in the gang, pay off corrupt police officials and distribute some welfare "goodies" to garrison residents to buy their assent and loyalty. Weapons are transhipped and pass through the Jamaican ports of entry in food barrels, car parts or hidden among construction equipment and materials. Money transfer services such as MoneyGram and Western Union are the preferred method through which Jamaicans in North America and the UK send cash to local dons. Stronger bilateral ties with Jamaican law enforcement and port authority officials are needed to disrupt the flow of weapons from north to south. Current policies such as limits on cash transactions and strict identification procedures must be maintained and expanded to restrict unbridled access to money by dons.

Future Research

Don Dada focused on one case, the garrison community of Brown Villa; however, the garrison and don phenomena transcend one geographic space in Jamaica. Based on the interviews with members of non-governmental and community-based organisations, the police and individuals who live and work outside Brown Villa, not all garrison communities have the same dynamics of don power and control. Additional research could investigate the specific characteristics of donmanship in communities outside the Kingston Metropolitan space. In the tourist city of Montego Bay in the western section of the island for example, a police report from the JCF indicates that gangs and dons in that area use the proceeds of a lottery-scam industry to fund their criminal enterprise (Bourne, Chambers, Blake, Sharpe-Pryce and Solan 2013).[11] This phenomenon should be of interest to scholars of transnational organised crime and international political economy.

Jamaican dons are the central unit of analysis in this study. While others have investigated the influence of dons on political, gang and garrison-related violence and homicides, the status and social power that dons have inside Jamaica's marginal communities seldom receive particular attention. This analysis should encourage other scholars with an interest in Jamaican politics and society to undertake detailed research on the specific phenomenon of dons. Previous scholars (Edie 1984, 1994; Sives 1998, 2002; Stone, 1985; Witter 1992) of comparative politics have explained the relationship among Jamaica's political parties, local dons, and garrison communities from the perspective of clientelism. The findings suggest it may now be useful to employ other analytic frames and theories to examine the influence these criminal non-state actors have had on the Jamaican state and society. This study employed the concept of embeddedness and theories of governance to interpret the status and localised authority dons have enjoyed in Jamaican garrison communities. Embeddedness has utility for scholars (particularly criminal anthropologists and comparative political scientists) conducting research in other geographic areas in the Americas. They may find it useful in interpreting the social, economic, or political relationships that criminal actors have with residents of local communities, the market, and state officials.

In addition, this study suggests the need for more research on the Caribbean region concerning the impact that illicit markets and rogue actors have on the processes of community development and governance. Violence tends to accompany drug and gun trading, extortion rackets and human trafficking. These problems confront all states in the region in different ways. Scholars need to know more about these varied contexts. It is also important that more comparative work be undertaken within the Caribbean region as well as in nations just beyond it (especially in Latin America) that face similar challenges. The Haitian-Jamaican guns-for-drugs and guns-for-food trade is an area that offers scope for future research on the influence that transnational illicit markets have on the security prospects of developing countries such as Jamaica.

No evidence of female dons emerged. However, some residents pointed out that women play important roles as caregivers to dons and their children. Women do assume important responsibilities inside the organisational structure of a gang. Police interviewees noted that dons often use women as drug mules (couriers) to tranship cocaine using international commercial flights from Kingston to various destinations in the US, Canada and the UK. There was no in-depth investigation into the roles women play in garrisons vis-á-vis dons and their gangs. Violence, organised crime, and gang activity are often portrayed as male-centred. There is room for an exploration of the connections between gender and organised crime to uncover how women contribute to the scope and nature of gang/don-related violence.

Conclusion

Since its independence in 1962, Jamaica has not had any major threat of democratic reversal or collapse. However, its adversarial partisan politics has had a deleterious effect on the institutions and culture of democratic governance. It is out of this insidious aspect of Jamaican politics that dons first emerged. In the decades after independence, dons have evolved into powerful governing actors. In many communities, they have supplanted or undermined the authority of the state. Jamaica's dons have managed to embed themselves within the socio-economic, cultural, and political fabric of life in garrison communities. The state, along with market institutions and civil society groups, must re-habituate and re-habilitate members of these communities. The social isolation and economic inequality so characteristic of garrison communities must be addressed and reversed. Although dons receive significant assent and popular support from residents, they rule with an iron fist that often militates against those individuals' civil and political rights and freedoms. If dons remain embedded, garrison residents should be prepared to accept the collateral damage of fear and violence that accompany the often-limited social welfare and security roles they offer. The state also should be prepared to operate inside these communities on terms set by dons/gangs if they are not dis-embedded.

Notes

Chapter One

1. See the Urban Dictionary's definition of Don Dada. Retrieved from https://www.urbandictionary.com/define.php?term=dondad.
2. The Jamaican Patwah: Patois and Slang Dictionary. Retrieved from https://jamaicanpatwah.com/term/Don-dada/1490#.XpnAmVNKjBI.
3. The term "garrison" was first used in the Jamaican context by Carl Stone (1985) to describe inner-city communities characterised by bounded political partisan loyalties among residents for either the Jamaican Labor Party (JLP) or the Peoples National Party (PNP). Violence of various sorts has long characterised these communities.
4. This phrase is used in Jamaica to refer to men considered to be dominant males on account of their sexual prowess, financial strength and the respect they have among their peers and within their communities. The phrase is popular among the lower middle and working class.
5. A yard in Jamaica refers to the physical living space of a home(s). In some inner-city and garrison communities, several families share one yard.
6. Over-voting refers to fraudulent patterns of voting in which there is more than a 100 per cent voter turnout in a constituency; ballots sometimes are cast for dead persons and one party tends to dominate electoral results, typically gaining more than 70 per cent of total votes reported.
7. The title "area leader" has a distinctly political partisan character; that is, these men have traditionally acted as intermediaries between the state (political parties) and residents of garrisons.
8. A copy of the report can be retrieved online at https://www.unodc.org/unodc/en/data-and-analysis/WDR-2008.html.
9. Griffith (1997 and 2004) contends that the Caribbean region's geography facilitates the rise of drug and gun trafficking. In his view, the mountainous topography of states like Haiti and Jamaica

facilitates clandestine drug operations (planting of marijuana and the construction of concealed airstrips).

10. The "glamour of ghetto" life in the Jamaican context involves the ownership of expensive cars, motorbikes, fashionable clothing, and jewellery, and for men, the "possession" of several women

11. These men were the infamous area leaders and dons of the Western Kingston garrison communities of Matthews Lane (Zekes) and Tivoli Gardens (Dudus). Both men are now incarcerated on drug, gun and murder-related charges. They were both feared and loved by residents of the garrisons they governed and each had strong associational ties to the two major political parties in Jamaica – Zekes to the PNP and Dudus to the JLP. I classify Zekes as an area don and Dudus as a mega don.

Chapter Two

1. Derived from information gathered from the Jamaica Constabulary Force [JCF] as well as from respondents interviewed within the JCF, NGOs and residents who work with community-based organisations (CBOs) in the research site under study.

2. Pseudonyms are used to identify those interviewed. A full list is provided in chapter four.

3. Article can be retrieved from the *Gleaner's* website at http://jamaica-gleaner.com/gleaner/20120112/lead/lead3.html.

4. Neoliberalism is a particular understanding of governance and what constitutes an appropriate relationship of capitalism and democratic institutions in a mixed political economy, which first attained prominence in the late 1970s and early 1980s. It argues for market-driven economies with minimal state involvement. In this research, I hypothesise that neoliberal programmes of Structural Adjustment Policies [SAPS] facilitated the embedding of dons in garrisons as the Jamaican state 'hollowed out' and grew increasingly weaker in its capacity to provide social and economic opportunities for its citizens, especially those residing in garrisons.

5. See Anthony Harriott's Inaugural Professorial Lecture, *The Challenge of Controlling Violence in Jamaica and the High Violence Societies of the Caribbean* (Arawak Publications, 24 April 2008). Harriott argued that a "subculture of violence" exists in Jamaica in which the gun is glorified. Similarly, several interview respondents pointed out that the gun is a symbol of power and control for the don and his foot soldiers (gang members) in garrisons.

6. This concept forms part of the analytical approach I use to interpret the power that dons have wielded in Jamaica's garrisons.

7. Retrieved from http://jamaica-gleaner.com/gleaner/20011211/cleisure/cleisure2.html.

8. In May 2010 the Jamaican state sent a joint military-police group into Tivoli Gardens, a garrison community in Western Kingston. The incursion was carried out to serve an extradition warrant request by the United States for then accused "drug lord" Christopher "Dudus" Coke on gun and drug trafficking charges. Coke was subsequently extradited to the US and is now incarcerated in the state of New York. Dudus became don of Tivoli Gardens in the 1990s. He took over as the don from his father Jim Brown, who had previously led the notorious "Showa Posse".

9. Retrieved from the *Gleaner* at http://jamaica-gleaner.com/gleaner/20110407/cleisure/cleisure3.html.

10. Statista's data on Jamaica's homicide over a six-year period (2014-2019) and on the larger Latin American region can be retrieved from https://www.statista.com/statistics/984761/homicide-rate-jamaica/#:~:text=Jamaica%3A%20homicide%20rate%202014%2D2019&text=In%202019%2C%20there%20were%20approximately,biggest%20rate%20reported%20in%202017.

11. See the National Report on Political Tribalism (1996) as well as the Task Force on Crime Report (2002). These accounts point out that 'political contracts' are a major source of funding for dons and their organised criminal gangs.

12. In their article, the authors argue that "security from below" (from non-state actors) is deemed more effective and legitimate than from above the state.

13. See the works of Johnson and Soeters (2008); and John Rapley (2003). These studies are among the few that make the don the central unit of analysis.

Chapter Three

1. Article can be retrieved from http://jamaica-gleaner.com/gleaner/20090612/lead/lead9.html.

2. Ibid.

3. A copy of the report is retrievable at http://news.bbc.co.uk/2/hi/americas/7684983.stm. The BBC published the account online on 25 October 2008.

4. See press release in the *Jamaica Observer*, 23 October 2020. Can be retrieved from http://www.jamaicaobserver.com/news/calling-all-dons-only-don-chuck-says-restorative-justice-helping-to-resolve-gang-issues_206063?profile=0.
5. As I have argued earlier in the book, garrisons are the social and geographic headquarters of Jamaica's organised crime mafia bosses and their syndicates.

Chapter Four

1. The Jamaican government established the SDC in 1965 as a state agency geared towards the development and self-governance of communities across the country. The SDC's approach to community development is built on research and social intervention. The agency works with several local and international groups such as the UNDP, USAID and the World Bank. In 2007, the SDC published community profiles of the neighbourhoods with which it is involved. For more information on the SDC, see http://www.sdc.gov.jm/home/.
2. CXC, the Caribbean Examinations Council, is a regional body in the English Caribbean that oversees and administers exams to secondary-level students. The CXC covers subjects in the humanities, arts and sciences [inclusive of math and English]. GCE 'O' Level is the British counterpart to CXC exams. Students are required to pass exams in five or more subjects including math and English in order to be eligible to matriculate for post-secondary education and training.
3. Retrieved from STATIN's website at http://statinja.gov.jm/LabourForce/UnemploymentRatesByAgeGroup.aspx.
4. The USD to JMD currency exchange rate stood at approximately JMD$85.50 to USD$1 in 2011 and in the first quarter of 2012 (Jan-Mar it was approximately JMD$87 to USD$1. Please see the World CIA Fact Book data at https://www.cia.gov/library/publications/the-world-factbook/geos/jm.html and the Bank of Jamaica website at http://www.boj.org.jm/foreign_exchange/fx_rates_monthly.php.
5. The Statistical Institute of Jamaica (STATIN) publishes the annual total employment by industry in large establishments for the entire country. These sectors are mining, manufacturing, electricity, gas and water, construction, trade, hotel and restaurants, transport, storage and communications, financing, insurance, real estate and business services, community, social and personal services

(including public education). STATIN data is available at http://statinja.gov.jm.

6. In *Persistent Poverty: Underdevelopment in Plantation Economies of the Third World* (1972), Beckford has argued that the plantation economy model instituted and adapted by most of the developing regions of the world serves to perpetuate poverty and underdevelopment. He contends that the plantation model is totalitarian, shaping not only the economy but also the political structure and social relations in society.

7. The term "foot soldier" describes a lower ranking "lieutenant" in a don's gang. Often, these individuals carry out the don's orders such as disciplining or punishing a community member deemed to be delinquent. They also execute robberies, extortion, murders, shootings and kidnapping on behalf of dons.

8. The Committee, comprised of elected officials, police, military, academic, business and civil society members, met in 1996 to discuss the problem of violence and political tribalism in Jamaica's garrison communities. The Honourable Justice James Kerr chaired the Committee.

9. Interviewee VT032 lives in a garrison community outside Brown Villa. In fact, the community in which he resides is located outside the Kingston and St Andrew metropolitan area. His views echo my own findings concerning dons and garrison communities in Jamaica.

10. Gunst (1995) in *Born Fi' Dead* explores how partisan battles between the Jamaican Labor Party and the Peoples National Party in Jamaica coincided with the trafficking and selling of cocaine and marijuana in several US cities in the 1980s, to create violent gangs and dons.

11. See http://www.nytimes.com/1990/12/08/nyregion/us-agents-seize-17-in-raids-to-dismantle-jamaican-drug-ring.html?pagewanted=all&src=pm.

12. Gunst (1995) has noted that this particular battle between the gangs from the two communities arose because of one don's anger over not receiving a construction contract.

13. Harriott (2008) is correct in his contention that Caribbean countries, including Jamaica, have developed sub-cultural values that normalise acts of violence, where the gun is glorified as a tool of power and respect among gang members.

14. Frances Madden's (2011) book *It's Not About Me: Working with Communities: Processes and Challenges*, presents some of her action-research work on life inside Jamaica's garrisons. She has

more than 30 years of experience working with residents in these neighbourhoods and has devised and employed several dispute-resolution strategies to engage some of the nation's dons and gangs.

Chapter Five

1. Retrieved from http://jamaica-gleaner.com/gleaner/20011211/cleisure/cleisure2.html.
2. Donna Hope in her work, *Inna Di Dancehall: Popular Culture and the Politics of Identity in Jamaica* (2006), has explored how dancehall culture, music and attitudes of masculinity and femininity are expressions of cultural identification in Jamaica, especially among its urban poor population.
3. HEART is a national training agency in Jamaica that offers several skills training certification courses in the areas of business, computer technologies, and auto-engineering.
4. This National Taskforce on Crime, also referred to as the Wolfe Report (1993), was convened to address the growing problem of violent crimes linked to inter-gang rivalries and political violence.
5. Several scholars have advanced this conceptualisation, including Figueroa (1992), *Garrison Communities in Jamaica 1962–1993: The Growth and Impact of Political Culture*; Witter (1992), *Patron Clientelism: Implications for Garrison Communities*. In 1992, the Kerr Report similarly portrayed governance of these communities as shadow versions of social ordering existing apart from and within the larger central authority of the state.
6. The reference to 'Babylon' is an analogy to the oppressive regime of the Babylonian Empires first founded in 1876 BC. Garrison residents frequently use "Babylon" to describe the oppressive and unequal treatment they receive from "official" Jamaican law enforcement officials.
7. Retrieved from *Jamaica Gleaner* at http://jamaica-gleaner.com/gleaner/20040208/focus/focus1.html.
8. These men were dons in garrison communities in the West Kingston area during the 1970s; they were strongly aligned with and supported by officials from the PNP or the JLP.
9. This interviewee operates a business in Brown Villa and is also the director of a social intervention CBO in the community. In his view, the don evolved from being a political enforcer in the 1970s to playing a central role as a "chief community welfare officer" in the decades after the 1980s; this role as chief welfare officer has

become largely the province of mega and area dons. As noted above, street dons rarely have the local and transnational network links to licit and illicit economies (such as drug trafficking, extortion rinks and mega robberies) to garner sufficient resources to play this role on a large scale.

10. The Urban Development Corporation (UDC) is a government agency established in 1968. Its primary responsibilities include overseeing and granting contracts to build and maintain public infrastructure, develop new townships and solve problems related to urban settlement. One of the major projects that the UDC oversees is the Inner-city Renewal Programme. NGO activists and other non-state actors have criticised the Jamaican Private Sector Organisation (PSOJ), which grants public contracts to carry out infrastructure work, for corruption and impropriety since the agency was created. See the UDC's website at http://www.udcja.com/ The PSOJ's website is accessibly at http://www.psoj.org/.

11. See the *Jamaica Gleaner* archives for articles and reports on the intensity of political violence during the 1980s. The following link from the Gleaner sheds some light on the political and social events of 1980 particularly, in Jamaica: http://jamaica-gleaner.com/gleaner/20010913/cleisure/cleisure1.html.

12. See Carl Stone's article in the *Jamaica Gleaner*, "A country playing with fire" 14 March 1990. Stone's various works explore the links among clientelism, electoral performance, political tribalism and democracy in the English-speaking Caribbean. His books include *Democracy and Clientelism in Jamaica* (1985).

13. "Don of dons", "real bad man", or "ghetto governor" are terms garrison residents used to describe their community leaders. These titles indicate the admiration and fear that residents have for these non-state actors. Obeika Gray, in *Demeaned But Empowered: The Social Power of the Urban Poor in Jamaica* (2004), argued that inside Jamaica's urban inner cities, the poor have constructed their social values and mores as a means of resistance to and rejection of an official state system that has failed to include them as equal citizens. He notes a "badness honour" inside some of these communities, in which the don and gangster cultures are more readily accepted.

14. Terry Lacey (1977) and later Obeika Gray (1994, 2004) have used the Marxist term "lumpenproletariat" to describe the urban poor who were social deviants and engaged in anti-system behaviours such as vandalism, looting and street rioting. Members of the elite

class, or what Lacey termed the national bourgeoisie in Jamaica in the 1960s, referred to many of the urban poor as the "hooligan" or "criminal" element of the urban working class.

15. This refers to the Cold War non-alliance movement in which some states took a stance of neutrality. The non-aligned countries mostly were states in the developing regions of the world.

16. Edward Seaga first proposed the idea in 1979. The Caribbean Basin Initiative was a 'Marshall Plan' tailor-made for the Caribbean and Central America. It united the two regions into a single strategic area. The objectives were that the region would benefit by having liberal access to US markets, stronger economic assistance, and greater incentives for investing capital. See too Anthony Maingot, (1994), *The United States and the Caribbean: Challenges of an Asymmetrical Relationship.*

17. Document can be retrieved at https://www.worldbank.org/en/news/feature/2011/06/23/new-world-bank-report-supports-jamaicas-efforts-to-unlockgrowth#:~:text=The%20World%20Bank%27s%20recent%20Country,quoted%20a%201952%20World%20Bank.

18. This is a multitask force comprised of Jamaican police and military personnel. Launched in October 2004, its main objective is to target the leaders of organised crime in Jamaica. The agency works closely with law enforcement allies in the United States, Canada and the UK.

19. Producer states' are those countries in the South American Andean Ridge that cultivate the coca plant, which is used to manufacture cocaine powder. These nations include Peru, Bolivia and Colombia.

20. Document can be retrieved online from the UNOC's website at http://www.unodc.org/documents/wdr/WDR_2010/1.3_The_globa_cocaine_market.pdf.

21. Newspaper and online reports from the BBC and NPR. See also the work of William O. Walker III. (1994) *Drug Trafficking in the Americas.*

22. CW-1 declared himself a senior member of the Shower Posse gang in the 1980s–1990s. The gang had its headquarters in the garrison of Tivoli Gardens, but it also had network branches in cities in the US Northeast. He said he worked as a personal bodyguard to the gang's leader and then don, Lester Lloyd "Jim Brown" Coke and later he performed the same role for Christopher Coke.

23. Nick Davis, "Haiti and Jamaica's deadly trade", available online news.bbc.co.uk/2/hi/Americas/7684983.stm.

24. The Cays lay outside the parish of Kingston Jamaica's National Environment and Planning Agency (NEPA) has designated the area as a special habitat for several species of birds and sea turtles.
25. This conversation took place on 16 November 2011. The conversation was not recorded. However, the information received helped to inform the field notes memo. Yellow's remarks were noted verbtim and cohered with information collected from senior police interviewees and from newspaper articles.
26. Ibid.
27. The report is online at http://www.state.gov/j/inl/rls/nrcrpt/2012/vol1/184099.htm#Haiti.
28. Ibid.
29. Article is online athttp://jamaica-gleaner.com/gleaner/20110614/lead/lead2.html. See also the work of Agozino, O., et al. (2009), *Guns, Crime and Social Order in the West Indies*; in it, the authors made note of the influence the Haitian-Jamaican trade had on the 'weaponisation' of the West Indies.
30. Retrieved online from the *Jamaica Observer* newspaper at http://www.jamaicaobserver.com/news/Complete-text-of-cooperating-witness-statement-against--Dudus.

Chapter Six

1. Borrowed from the work of Vadim Volkov (2002), *Violent Entrepreneurs: The Use of Force in the Making of Russian Capitalism*. Volkov contends that criminal groups, private security firms and the state have all used 'organised force' and 'managed violence' to create a new market-driven economy in post-Soviet Russia. His analysis illustrated how non-state criminal groups may be integrated into the political economy of the state and society.
2. Interviewees used these phrases to describe garrison dons. Respondents included community residents, journalists and directors of local NGOs that work in the garrison (including Brown Villa).
3. Report from the Social Development Commission's (SDC) Community Profile assessment for Brown Villa 2011.
4. Barry Chevannes's (2002) work, *What You Sow is What You Reap: Violence and the Construction of Male Identity in Jamaica* provides more insight into the ways in which Jamaican manhood and masculinity have been defined within urban inner-city garrison

contexts. He argued that boys often view dons and gang members as folk heroes and community icons. Adam Baird (2012) in his article, "The Violent Gang and the Construction of Masculinity Amongst Socially Excluded Young Men" has also explored the connection between masculinity and youth involvement in violence. His work chronicles the phenomenon in Colombia.

5. Matthews Lane is a community in the West Kingston division of the capital city, Kingston. Donald "Zekes" Phipps was a mega don comparable to Christopher "Dudus" Coke. In fact, during the 1990s, these individuals divided the Downtown Kingston business district between themselves for purposes of extortion and protection rackets.

6. The New York Daily News article by Helen Peterson (1 May 1997) "Drug suspect's run ended" gives a snapshot of the enormous wealth Vassell and his 'Gullymen' gang acquired from the narcotics trade. It also shows the violence associated with the illicit trade. The article can be retrieved at http://articles.nydailynews.com/1997-05-01/local/18039648_1_drug-trafficking-charges-drug-ring-crown-heights.

7. See the work of Michael Collier (2005), *Political Corruption in the Caribbean Basin: Constructing a Theory to Combat Corruption.* He explores in depth the causal mechanisms for and results of political corruption in the Caribbean region.

8. Horace Levy (2009), in his work Killing Streets and Community Revival used this term to differentiate among garrison-type gangs, which tend to be more organised than street gangs and usually have a distinct chain of command in terms of leadership. Street gangs and corner crews are lower down the social scale of Jamaican gangs, with corner crews being loosely organised groups of young men with limited access to weapons.

9. See newspaper report from the Jamaica Observer retrieved from http://www.jamaicaobserver.com/front-page/goats-stolen-to-fund-gangs-clarendon-police-move-to-curtail-growing-practice-of-new-meat-for-guns-trade_143147?profile=&template=PrinterVersion.

10. The Law Reform (Zones of Special Operation) (Special Security and Community Development Measures) Act was passed in the Jamaican parliament in 2017. See article from the Jamaica Observer that explains the origins of the Bill and its implications for citizen rights in communities where the security measure of crime and violence control has been used. Retrieved from http://www.

jamaicaobserver.com/news/states-of-emergency-zozos-and-states-of-emergency-zozos-and-the-fundamental_154611?profile=1096.

11. Since 2006, lottery scams have developed in Jamaica, involving the country's call centre database to defraud US citizens of cash. Blake (2018) discussed how lotto scamming is fuelling gang wars in Jamaica. See article retrieved from https://theconversation.com/how-lotto-scammers-defraud-elderly-americans-and-fuel-gang-wars-in-jamaica-90676. See also David McFadden's article, "Jamaica lottery scam: 8 fraud suspects arrested" (17 May 2012) in the Huffington Post at the following online link for some background information: http://www.huffingtonpost.com/2012/05/17/jamaica-lottery-scam-fraud-suspects-arrested_n_1525498.html.

References

Aberbach, Joel D., and Bert A. Rockman. 2002. "Conducting and Coding Elite Interviews." *Ps, Political Science & Politics* 35 (4): 673–76.

Agozino, Biko, Ben Bowling, Elizabeth Ward, and Godfrey St Bernard. 2009. "Guns, Crime and Social Order in the West Indies." *Criminology & Criminal Justice* 9 (3): 287–305.

Amnesty International. 2008. "Jamaica: Gang and Police Violence in the Inner Cities." *Amnesty International* 38.

Appadurai, Arjun. 2004. "The Capacity to Aspire: Culture and the Terms of Recognition." In *Culture and Public Action*, edited by Vijayendra Rao and Michael Walton, 59–84. Stanford, CA: Stanford University Press.

Arendt, Hannah. 1968. *Between Past and Future: Eight Exercises in Political Thought*. New York, NY: Viking Press.

Arias, Enrique Desmond. 2017. *Criminal Enterprises and Governance in Latin America and the Caribbean*. Cambridge: Cambridge University Press.

Auerbach, Carl F., and Louise B. Silverstein. 2003. *Qualitative Data: An Introduction to Coding and Analysis*. New York, NY: New York University Press.

Baird, Adam. 2012. "The Violent Gang and the Construction of Masculinity amongst Socially Excluded Young Men." *Safer Communities* 11 (4): 179–90.

Barzel, Yoram. 2002. *A Theory of the State: Economic Rights, Legal Rights, and the Scope of the State*. Cambridge: Cambridge University Press.

Baum, Dan. 1997. *Smoke and Mirrors: The War on Drugs and the Politics of Failure*. Boston, MA: Back Bay Books.

Baxter, Pamela, and Susan Jack. 2008. "Qualitative Case Study Methodology: Study Design and Implementation for Novice Researchers." *Qualitative Report* 13 (4): 544–59.

Beck, Ulrich. 2005. *Power in the Global Age: A New Global Political Economy*. Cambridge: Polity.

Beckford, George L. 1972. *Persistent Poverty: Underdevelopment in Plantation Economies of the Third World*. New York, NY: Oxford University Press.

Beetham, David, and Kevin Boyle. 1995. *Introducing Democracy: 80 Questions and Answers*. Cambridge: Polity Press.

Bell, Stephen, and Andrew Hindmoor. 2009. *Rethinking Governance: The Centrality of the State in Modern Society*. Cambridge: Cambridge University Press.

Bertram, Eva. 1996. *Drug War Politics: The Price of Denial*. Berkeley, CA: University of California Press.

Best, Lloyd, and Selwyn D. Ryan. 2003. *Independent Thought and Caribbean Freedom: Essays in Honour of Lloyd Best*. St Augustine, Trinidad and Tobago: Sir Arthur Lewis Institute of Social and Economic Studies.

Bevir, Mark. 2010. *Democratic Governance*. Princeton, NJ: Princeton University Press.

Blake, Damion. 2013. "Shadowing the State: Violent Control and the Social Power of Jamaican Garrison Dons." *Journal of Ethnographic & Qualitative Research* 8 (1): 56–75.

———. 2020. "Researching Violence: Conducting Risky Fieldwork in Dangerous Spaces across Latin America and the Caribbean." *Journal of Ethnographic & Qualitative Research* 14 (3): 153–69.

Blake, Damion Keith. 2004. "Direct Democracy and the New Paradigm of Democratic Politics in Jamaica." *Social and Economic Studies* 53 (4): 163–90.

Blake, Duane. 2003. *Shower Posse: The Most Notorious Jamaican Criminal Organization*. New York, NY: Diamond Publishers.

Bourdieu, Pierre. 1986. "Forms of Capital." In *Handbook of Theory and Research for the Sociology of Education*, edited by John Richardson, 241–58. New York, NY: Greenwood Press.

Bourne, Paul Andrew, Chad Chambers, Damion K. Blake, Charlene Sharpe-Pryce, and Ikhalfani Solan. 2013. "Lottery Scam in a Third-World Nation: The Economics of a Financial Crime and Its Breadth." *Asian Journal of Business Management* 5 (1): 19–51.

Bourne, Paul, Damion Blake, Charlene Sharpe-Pryce, and Ikhalfani Solan. 2014. "Murder and Politics in Jamaica: A Historical

Quantitative Analysis, 1970–2009." *Asian Journal of Business Management* 4 (3): 233–51.

Bowling, Benjamin. 2010. *Policing the Caribbean: Transnational Security Cooperation in Practice*. Oxford: Oxford University Press.

Boyne, Ian. 2004. "De-linking Politics and Crime." *The Jamaican Gleaner*. February 8. https://old.jamaica-gleaner.com/gleaner/20040208/focus/focus1.html.

Briggs, Xavier de Souza. 2008. *Democracy as Problem Solving: Civic Capacity in Communities Across the Globe*. Cambridge, MA: MIT Press.

Briquet, Jean-Louis, and Gilles Favarel-Garrigues. 2010. *Organized Crime and States: The Hidden Face of Politics*. New York, NY: Palgrave Macmillan.

Calvet, Martin Sanzana, and Vanesa Castan Broto. "Neoliberal shock, infrastructure disruption, and restructuring in Chile." *Critical Planning* 22 (2015) https://escholarship.org/uc/item/2b572861.

Campbell, Yonique. 2020. *Citizenship on the Margins: State Power, Security and Precariousness in 21st-Century Jamaica*. Studies of the Americas. Cham, Switzerland: Palgrave Macmillan.

Caribbean Human Development Report. 2012. *Human Development and the Shift to Better Citizen Security*. New York, NY: United Nations Development Program.

Carranza, Camilo, and Chris Dalby. 2019. In-Sight Crime's 2018 Homicide Round-Up. *In-Sight Crime*.

Castells, Manuel. 1996. *The Rise of the Network Society*. Malden, MA: Blackwell Publishers.

———. 2000. *End of Millennium*. 2nd ed. Oxford: Blackwell Publishers.

———, and Gustavo Cardoso. 2006. *The Network Society: From Knowledge to Policy*. Washington, DC: Centre for Transatlantic Relations, Paul H. Nitze School of Advanced International Studies: Johns Hopkins University.

Charles, Christopher A.D. 2004. "Political Identity and Criminal Violence in Jamaica: The Garrison Community of August Town and the 2002 Election." *Social and Economic Studies* 53 (2): 31–73.

Chevannes, Barry. 1981. "The Rastafari and the Urban Youth." In *Perspectives on Jamaica in the1970s*, edited by Carl Stone, 392–422. Kingston, Jamaica: Jamaica Publishing House.

———. 1992. "The Formation of Garrison Communities." Paper presented at the Symposium, Grassroots Development and the State of the Nation. University of the West Indies, Mona Campus, November 16–17.

———. 2002. "What you Sow is What you Reap: Violence and the Construction of Male Identity in Jamaica." *Current Issues in Comparative Education* 2 (1).

Chotray, Vasudha. 2009. *Governance Theory and Practice: A Cross-disciplinary Approach*. New York: Palgrave Macmillan.

Clarke, Colin. 1991. *Society and Politics in the Caribbean*. New York, NY: St. Martin's Press.

———. 2006. "Politics, Violence and Drugs in Kingston, Jamaica." *Bulletin of Latin American Research* 25 (3): 420–40.

Colak, Alexandra Abello, and Jenny Pearce. 2009. "'Security from below' in Contexts of Chronic Violence." *Ids Bulletin* 40 (2): 11–19.

Coles, Tony. 2009. "Negotiating the Field of Masculinity: The Production and Reproduction of Multiple Dominant Masculinities." *Men and Masculinities* 12 (1): 30–44.

Collier, Michael. 2005. *Political Corruption in the Caribbean Basin Constructing a Theory to Combat Corruption*. New York, NY: Routledge.

Connell, R.W. 1987. *Gender and Power: Society, the Person, and Sexual Politics*. Cambridge: Polity in association with Blackwell.

Cooper, Carolyn. 1995. *Noises in the Blood: Orality, Gender, and the "Vulgar" Body of Jamaican Popular Culture*. Durham, NC: Duke University Press.

———. 2004. *Sound Clash: Jamaican Dancehall Culture at Large*. 1st ed. New York, NY: Palgrave Macmillan.

Covey, Herbert. 2003. *Street Gangs Throughout the World*. Springfield, MA: Charles C. Thomas.

Cudworth, Erika, Timothy Hall, and John McGovern. 2007. *The Modern State: Theories and Ideologies*. Edinburgh: Edinburgh University Press.

Dahl, Robert A. 1998. *On Democracy*. New Haven, CT: Yale University Press.

Davis, Mike, and Daniel Bertrand Monk. 2007. *Evil Paradises: Dreamworlds of Neoliberalism*. New York, NY: New Press.

Davis, Nick. 2008. "Haiti and Jamaica's Deadly Trade." *BBC News*.

Decker, Scott H., and Margaret Townsend Chapman. 2008. *Drug Smugglers on Drug Smuggling: Lessons from the Inside*. Philadelphia, PA: Temple University Press.

DeMars, William E. 2005. *NGOs and Transnational Networks: Wild Cards in World Politics*. London; Ann Arbor, MI: Pluto Press.

Desch, Michael C., Jorge I. Domínguez, and Serbín Andrés. 1998. *From Pirates to Drug Lords: The Post-Cold War Caribbean Security Environment*. Albany, NY: State University of New York Press.

Diamond, Larry Jay, Leonardo Morlino, and American Political Science Association. 2005. *Assessing the Quality of Democracy*. Baltimore, MD: Johns Hopkins University Press.

Domínguez Jorge I., Robert A. Pastor, and DeLisle Worrell. 1993. *Democracy in the Caribbean: Political, Economic, and Social Perspectives*. Baltimore, MD: Johns Hopkins University Press.

Domínguez, Jorge. 1998. *International Security and Democracy: Latin America and the Caribbean in the Post-Cold War Era*. Pittsburgh, PA: University of Pittsburgh Press.

Dryzek, John S. 2006. *Deliberative Global Politics: Discourse and Democracy in a Divided World*. Cambridge: Polity.

Duffy, Rosaleen. 2010. "Shadow States: Globalization, Criminalization, and Environmental Change." In *Organized Crime and States: The Hidden Face of Politics*, edited by Jean-Louis Briquet and Gilles Favarel-Garrigues, 97–116. New York, NY: Palgrave Macmillan.

Edie, Carlene J. 1984. "Dual Dependency: Patron-clientelist Relations in Jamaica." Doctoral Dissertation. University of California.

———. 1989. "From Manley to Seaga: The Persistence of Clientelist Politics in Jamaica." *Social and Economic Studies* 38 (1): 1–35.

———. 1991. *Democracy by Default: Dependency and Clientelism in Jamaica*. Kingston, Jamaica: Ian Randle Publishers.

———. 1994. *Democracy in the Caribbean: Myths and Realities*. Westport, CT: Prager Publishers.

Edmonds, Kevin. 2016. "Guns, Gangs and Garrison Communities in the Politics of Jamaica." *Race & Class* 57 (4): 54–74.

Eisenstadt, S.N., and Louis Roniger. 1980. "Patron-Client Relations as a Model of Structuring Social Exchange." *Comparative Studies in Society and History* 22 (1): 42–77.

Eisenstadt, Shemuel N. 1981. *Political Clientelism, Patronage, and Development*. Beverly Hills, CA: Sage Publications.

Erikson, Daniel P., and Adam Minson. 2005. "The Caribbean: Democracy Adrift?" *Journal of Democracy* 16 (4): 159–71.

Evans, Peter B., Dietrich Rueschemeyer, and Theda Skocpol. 1985. *Bringing the State Back In*. Cambridge: Cambridge University Press.

Eyre, L. Alan. 1984. "Political Violence and Urban Geography in Kingston, Jamaica." *Geographical Review* 74 (1): 24–37.

Favarel-Garrigues, Gilles. 2010. "Mafia Violence and Political Power in Russia." In *Organized Crime and States: The Hidden Face of Politics*, edited by Jean-Louis Briquet and Gilles Favarel-Garrigues, 147–72. New York, NY: Palgrave Macmillan.

Figueroa, M. 1996. *Garrison Communities in Jamaica 1962–1993: Their Growth and Impact on Political Culture*. Kingston, Jamaica: Sir Arthur Lewis Institute of Social and Economic Studies.

Figueroa, Michael. 1992. "Garrison Communities in Jamaica 1962–1993: The Growth and Impact of Political Culture." Paper presented at the Symposium, Grassroots Development and the State of the Nation. University of the West Indies, Mona, Jamaica.

Foner, Nancy. 1973. "Party Politics in a Jamaican Community." *Caribbean Studies* 13 (2): 51–64.

Friman, H. Richard, and Peter Andreas. 1999. *The Illicit Global Economy and State Power*. Lanham, MD: Rowman & Littlefield Publishers.

Gambetta, Diego. 1993. *The Sicilian Mafia: The Business of Private Protection*. Cambridge, MA: Harvard University Press.

Gellner, Ernest, and John Waterbury. 1977. *Patrons and Clients in Mediterranean Societies*. London: Duckworth.

Ghezzi, Simone, and Enzo Mingione. 2007. "Embeddedness, Path Dependency and Social Institutions." *Current Sociology* 55 (1): 11–23.

Giroux, Henry A. 2008. *Against the Terror of Neoliberalism: Politics Beyond the Age of Greed*. Boulder, CO: Paradigm Publishers.

Goldstein, Herman. 1977. *Policing a Free Society*. Cambridge, MA: Ballinger Pub. Co.

Gootenberg, Paul. 2009. *Andean Cocaine: The Making of a Global Drug*. Chapel Hill, NC: University of North Carolina Press.

Gorgan, W. 2012. "The Reintegration of Tivoli Gardens." *Jamaica Gleaner*. January 12. Retrieved from http://jamaica-gleaner.com/gleaner/20120112/lead/lead3.html.

Gottdiener, Mark. 1987. *The Decline of Urban Politics: Political Theory and the Crisis of the Local State*. Newbury Park, CA: Sage Publications.

Gounev, Philip, and Vincenzo Ruggiero. 2012. *Corruption and Organized Crime in Europe: Illegal Partnerships*. London: Routledge.

Granovetter, Mark. 1983. "The Strength of Weak Ties: A Network Theory Revisited." *Sociological Theory* 1, 201–33.

Gray, Obika. 1994. "Discovering the Social Power of the Poor." *Social and Economic Studies* 43 (3): 169–89.

———. 2003. "Predation Politics and the Political Impasse in Jamaica." *Small Axe: A Caribbean Journal of Criticism* 7 (1): 72–94.

———. 2004. *Demeaned but Empowered: The Social Power of the Urban Poor in Jamaica.* Kingston, Jamaica: University of the West Indies Press.

Griffith, Ivelaw. 1997. *Drugs and Security in the Caribbean: Sovereignty under Siege.* University Park, Pennsylvania: Pennsylvania State University Press.

———. 2004. *Caribbean Security in the Age of Terror: Challenge and Change.* Kingston, Jamaica: Ian Randle Publishers.

Griffith, I.L., and T. Munroe. 1996. "Drugs and Democracy in the Caribbean." *Journal of Commonwealth and Comparative Politics* 33 (3): 357–76.

Gunst, Laurie. 1995. *Born fi' Dead: A Journey through the Jamaican Posse Underworld.* New York, NY: H. Holt.

Hall, Stuart. 1978. *Policing the Crisis: Mugging, the State, and Law and Order.* London: Macmillan.

Harrell, Adele, and George. E. Peterson. 1992. *Drugs, Crime, and Social Isolation: Barriers to Urban Opportunity.* Washington, DC: Urban Institute Press.

Harriott, Anthony. 1996. "The Changing Social Organization of Crime and Criminals in Jamaica." *Caribbean Quarterly* 42 (2–3): 61–81.

———. 2000. *Police and Crime Control in Jamaica: Problems of Reforming Ex-Colonial Constabularies.* Kingston, Jamaica: University of the West Indies Press.

———. 2004. "The Jamaican Crime Problem: Some Policy Considerations." In *Crime and Criminal Justice in Jamaica*, edited by Farley Brathwaite, Anthony Harriott, Scot Wortley, 129–72. Kingston, Jamaica: Arawak Publishers.

———. 2004. *Understanding Crime in Jamaica: New Challenges for Public Policy.* Kingston, Jamaica: University of the West Indies Press.

———. 2008. *Bending the Trend Line: The Challenge of Controlling Violence in Jamaica and the High Violence Societies of the Caribbean.* Kingston, Jamaica: Arawak.

———. 2011. "The Emergence and Evolution of Organized Crime in Jamaica: New Challenges to Law Enforcement and Society." *West Indian Law Journal* 36 (2): 3–28.

Harris, Richard L. 2005. *Globalization and Development in Latin America*. Whitby, ON: De Sitter.

Hart, Richard. 1998. *From Occupation to Independence: A Short History of the Peoples of the English-speaking Caribbean Region*. London: Pluto Press.

Harvey, David. 2005. *A Brief History of Neoliberalism*. Oxford; New York, NY: Oxford University Press.

———. 2002. *A Spade is Still a Spade: Essays on Crime and the Politics of Jamaica*. Kingston, Jamaica: LMH Publishers.

Held, David. 2000. "Regulating Globalization? The Reinvention of Politics." *International Sociology* 15 (2): 394–408.

Henry-Lee, Aldrie. 2005. "The Nature of Poverty in the Garrison Constituencies in Jamaica." *Environment and Urbanization* 17 (2): 83–99.

Hillman, Richard S., and Thomas. J. D'Agostino. 2003. *Understanding the Contemporary Caribbean*. Boulder, CO: L. Rienner.

Hindess, Barry. 1996. *Discourses of Power: From Hobbes to Foucault*. Hoboken, NJ: Wiley.

Holston, James. 2008. *Insurgent Citizenship: Disjunctions of Democracy and Modernity in Brazil*. Princeton, NJ: Princeton University Press.

Hope, Donna. P. 2006. *Inna di Dancehall: Popular Culture and the Politics of Identity in Jamaica*. Kingston, Jamaica: University of the West Indies Press.

International Narcotics Control Strategy Report (INSCR). 1980. Washington, DC: US Department of State.

———. 2010. Washington, DC: US Department of State.

———. 2011. Washington, DC: US Department of State.

———. 2012. Washington, DC: US Department of State.

Jaffe, Rivke. 2019. "Writing around Violence: Representing Organized Crime in Kingston, Jamaica." *Ethnography* 20 (3): 379–96.

Johnson, Hume. 2005. "Incivility: The Politics of People on the Margins in Jamaica." *Political Studies* 53 (3): 579–97.

Johnson, Hume N., and Joseph L. Soeters. 2008. "Jamaican Dons, Italian Godfathers and the Chances of a 'Reversible Destiny.'" *Political Studies* 56 (1): 166–91.

Johnston, Jake, and Juan Montecino. 2011. *Jamaica: Macroeconomic Policy, Debt and the IMF*. Washington, DC: Centre for Economic and Policy Research.

Jones, Gareth A., and Dennis Rodgers. 2009. *Youth Violence in Latin America: Gangs and Juvenile Justice in Perspective*. New York, NY: Palgrave Macmillan.

Jones, Marlyn J. 2002. "Policy Paradox: Implications of U.S. Drug Control Policy for Jamaica." *The ANNALS of the American Academy of Political and Social Science* 582 (1): 117–33.

Kahler, Miles, and David A. Lake. 2004. "Governance in a Global Economy: Political Authority in Transition." *PS: Political Science and Politics* 37 (3): 409–14.

Kiewiet, D. Roderick, and Mathew Daniel McCubbins. 1991. *The Logic of Delegation: Congressional Parties and the Appropriations Process*. Chicago, IL: University of Chicago Press.

Kitthananan, Amornsak. 2006. "Conceptualizing Governance: A Review." *Journal of Societal & Social Policy* 5 (3): 1–19.

Klak, Thomas. 1992. "Excluding the Poor from Low Income Housing Programs: The Roles of State Agencies and USAID in Jamaica." *Antipode* 24 (2): 87–112.

———. 1998. *Globalization and Neoliberalism: The Caribbean Context*. Lanham, MD: Rowman & Littlefield.

———. 1999. "Globalization, Neoliberalism and Economic Change in Central America and the Caribbean." In *Latin America Transformed: Globalization and Modernity*, edited by Robert N. Gwynne and Kay Cristóbal, 98–126. London: Edward Arnold Publishers.

———, and Garth Myers. 1997. "The Discursive Tactics of Neoliberal Development in Small Third World Countries." *Geoforum* 28 (2): 133–49.

Klein, Axel, Marcus Day, and Anthony Harriot. 2004. *Caribbean Drugs: From Criminalization to Harm Reduction*. Kingston, Jamaica: Ian Randle Publishers.

Klein, Naomi. 2007. *The Shock Doctrine: The Rise of Disaster Capitalism*. New York, NY: Metropolitan Books/Henry Holt.

Koonings, Kees, and Dirk Kruijt. 2007. *Fractured Cities: Social Exclusion, Urban Violence and Contested Spaces in Latin America*. London: Zed Books.

Lacey, Terry. 1977. *Violence and Politics in Jamaica 1960–70: Internal Security in a Developing Country*. Manchester: Manchester University Press.

Langley, Ann. 1999. "Strategies for Theorizing from Process Data." *The Academy of Management Review* 24 (4): 691–710.

Le Franc, E., M. Samms-Vaughan, I. Hambleton, K. Fox, and D. Brown. 2008. "Interpersonal Violence in Three Caribbean Countries: Barbados, Jamaica and Trinidad and Tobago." *Pan America Journal of Public Health* 24 (6): 409–21.

Leslie, Glaister. 2010. *Confronting the Don the Political Economy of Gang Violence in Jamaica*. Geneva, Switzerland: Small Arms Survey.

Levy, Horace. 2009. *Killing Streets and Community Revival*. Kingston, Jamaica: Arawak Publications.

———, and University of the West Indies. 1996. *They Cry Respect: Urban Violence and Poverty in Jamaica*. Kingston, Jamaica: Centre for Population, Community and Social Change, Department of Sociology and Social Work, University of the West Indies, Mona.

Lindsay, Louis. 1975. *The Myth of Independence: Middle Class Politics and Non-mobilization in Jamaica*. Mona, Jamaica: Institute of Social and Economic Research, University of the West Indies.

Luker, Kristin. 2008. *Salsa Dancing into the Social Sciences: Research in an Age of Info-glut*. Cambridge, MA: Harvard University Press.

Mackie, Erin Skye. 2005. "Welcome the Outlaw: Pirates, Maroons, and Caribbean Countercultures." *Cultural Critique* 59 (1): 24–62.

Madden, Frances, and GraceKennedy Foundation. 2011. *"It's Not About Me": Working with Communities: Processes and Challenges*. The Grace and Staff Community Development Foundation Experience. Kingston, Jamaica: Grace Kennedy Foundation.

Maingot, Anthony. P. 1994. *The United States and the Caribbean: Challenges of an Asymmetrical Relationship*. Boulder, CO: Westview Press.

Manley, Michael. 1982. *Jamaica: Struggle in the Periphery*. London: Third World Media.

Manning, Paul. 2007. *Drugs and Popular Culture: Drugs, Media and Identity in Contemporary Society*. Devon: Willan Publishing.

Marez, Curtis. 2004. *Drug Wars: The Political Economy of Narcotics*. Minneapolis, MN: University of Minnesota Press.

Marshall, Martin. 1996. "Sampling for Qualitative Research." *Family Practice* 13 (6): 522–26.

Marx, Karl, and Friedrich Engels. 1967. *Capital: A Critique of Political Economy*. New York, NY: International.

Michels, Robert. 1999. *Political Parties: A Sociological Study of the Oligarchical Tendencies of Modern Democracy*. New York, NY: Dover Publications.

Moody, James, and Douglas R. White. 2003. "Structural Cohesion and Embeddedness: A Hierarchical Concept of Social Groups." *American Sociological Review* 68 (1): 103–27.

Montgomery, James D. 1998. "Toward a Role-Theoretic Conception of Embeddedness." *American Journal of Sociology* 104 (1): 92–125.

Moser, Caroline. 1998. "The Asset Vulnerability Framework: Reassessing Urban Poverty Reduction Strategies." *World Development* 26 (1): 1–19.

Moser, Caroline O.N., and Brookings Institution. 2006. *Reducing Urban Violence in Developing Countries*. Washington, DC: Brookings Institution.

Moser, Caroline O.N., and Jeremy Holland. 1997. *Urban Poverty and Violence in Jamaica*. Washington, DC: World Bank.

Moser, Caroline O.N., Cathy McIlwaine, and World Bank. 2001. *Violence in a Post-Conflict Context: Urban Poor Perceptions from Guatemala*. Washington, DC: World Bank.

Munroe, Michelle A., and Damion K. Blake. 2017. "Governance and Disorder: Neoliberalism and Violent Change in Jamaica." *Third World Quarterly* 38 (3): 580–603.

Munroe, Trevor. 1990. *Jamaican Politics: A Marxist Perspective in Transition*. Princeton, NJ: Princeton University Press.

———. 1999. *Renewing Democracy into the Millennium: The Jamaican Experience in Perspective*. Kingston, Jamaica: University of the West Indies Press.

National Committee on Political Tribalism, and J. S. Kerr. 1997. *Report of the National Committee on Political Tribalism*. Kingston, Jamaica: Jamaica Information Service.

Naylor, R.T. 2002. *Wages of Crime: Black Markets, Illegal Finance, and the Underworld Economy*. Ithaca, NY: Cornell University Press.

Nettleford, Rex M. 1998. *Mirror, Mirror: Identity, Race and Protest in Jamaica*. Kingston, Jamaica: Kingston Publishers Limited.

Nozick, Robert. 1974. *Anarchy, State, and Utopia*. New York, NY: Basic Books.

Ong, Aihwa. 2006. *Neoliberalism as Exception: Mutations in Citizenship and Sovereignty*. Durham, NC: Duke University Press.

Pareto, Vilfredo, and S.E. Finer. 1976. *Sociological Writings*. Totowa, NJ: Rowman and Littlefield.

Patton, Michael Q. 1990. *Qualitative Evaluation and Research Methods*. Newbury Park, CA: Sage Publications.

———. 2002. *Qualitative Research and Evaluation Methods*. Thousand Oaks, CA: Sage Publications.

Payne Anthony. 1995. *Politics in Jamaica*. Rev. ed. New York: St. Martin's Press.

Pereira, A.W., and D. Davis. 2000. "New Patterns of Militarized Violence in the Americas." *Latin American Perspectives* 27 (2): 3–17.

Pierre, Jon. 2000. *Debating Governance: Authenticity, Steering, and Democracy*. Oxford: Oxford University Press.

———, and B. Guy Peters. 2020. *Governance Politics and the State*. 2nd ed. London: Red Globe Press.

Powell, Lawrence, and Balford Lewis. 2011. *The Political Culture of Democracy in Jamaica: Democratic Consolidation in the Americas in Hard Times*. Kingston, Jamaica: The University of the West Indies; Nashville, TN: Vanderbilt University.

Powell, Lawrence A., Paul Bourne, and Lloyd Waller. 2007. *Probing Jamaica's Political Culture: Main Trends in the July–August 2006 Leadership Governance Survey. Volume 1*. Kingston, Jamaica: Centre for Leadership and Governance, University of the West Indies.

———, Robert Leonardi, and Raffaella Y. Nanetti. 1993. *Making Democracy Work: Civic Traditions in Modern Italy*. Princeton, NJ: Princeton University Press.

Rao, Vijayendra, and Michael Walton. 2004. *Culture and Public Action*. Stanford, CA: Stanford University Press.

Rapley, John. 2004. *Globalization and Inequality: Neoliberalism's Downward Spiral*. Boulder, CO: Lynne Rienner.

———. 2003. "Jamaica: Negotiating Law and Order with the Dons." *Crime, Disorder and Policing* 37 (2): 25–29.

Rattary, Garth. 2001. "The Origins and Roles of Dons." *Jamaica Gleaner*.

Raven, Bertram H., and John R.P. French, Jr. 1958. "Legitimate Power, Coercive Power, and Observability in Social Influence." *Sociometry* 21 (2): 83–97.

Rawls, John. 1971. *A Theory of Justice*. Cambridge, MA: Belknap Press of Harvard University Press.

Report of the National Committee on Crime and Violence. 2002. *Report of the National Committee on Crime and Violence*. Kingston, Jamaica: Jamaica Information Service.

Report of the National Taskforce on Crime and L. Wolfe. 1993. *Report of the National Taskforce on Crime*. Kingston, Jamaica: Jamaica Information Service.

Report of the Special Taskforce on Crime. 2006. *Road Map to a Safe and Secure Jamaica*. Kingston, Jamaica: Jamaica Information Service.

Rhodes, R.A.W. 1994. "The Hollowing Out of the State: The Changing Nature of the Public Service in Britain." *Political Quarterly* 65 (2): 138–51.

———. 2000. "The Governance Narrative: Key Findings and Lessons from the ERC's Whitehall Programme." *Public Administration* 78 (2): 345–63.

Robotham, Don. 2003. "Crime and Public Policy in Jamaica." In *Understanding Crime in Jamaica: New Challenges for Public Policy*, edited by Anthony Harriott, 197–238. Kingston, Jamaica: University of the West Indies Press.

Rodgers, Dennis, and Steffen Jensen. 20009: "Revolutionaries, Barbarians or War Machines? Gangs in Nicaragua and South Africa." *Socialist Register* 45:220–38.

Rosenau, J.N. 2000. *Governance without Government: Order and Change in World Politics*. Cambridge, UK: Cambridge University Press.

Rosenau, Pauline Vaillancourt, ed. 2000. *Public-private Policy Partnerships*. Boston, MA: MIT Press.

Rossman, Gretchen B., and Sharon F. Rallis. 2003. *Learning in the Field: An Introduction to Qualitative Research*. Thousand Oaks, CA: Sage Publications.

Rowden, Rick. 2009. *The Deadly Ideas of Neoliberalism*. New York: Zed Books.

Ruggiero, Vincenzo. 2002. "Introduction – Fuzzy Criminal Actors." *Crime Law and Social Change* 37 (3): 177–90.

———. 2010. "Who Corrupts Whom? A Criminal Eco-system Made in Italy." *Crime, Law and Social Change* 54 (1): 87–105. https://doi.org/10.1007/s10611-010-9242-9.

Ryan, Selwyn. 1999. *Winner Takes All: The Westminster Experience in the Anglophone Caribbean*. St Augustine, Trinidad and Tobago: I.S.E.R.

Samper, Jota. 2016. "Urban Upgrading in a Context of Violence: Perceptions of Security and Physical Space in the Case of the Favela-Bairro in Rio de Janeiro." *International Relations and Diplomacy* 4 (12): 760–78.

Sandel, Michael. 1996. *Democracy's Discontent: America in Search of a Public Philosophy*. Cambridge, MA: Belknap Press of Harvard University Press.

Schendel, Willem van, and Itty Abraham. 2005. *Illicit Flows and Criminal Things: States, Borders, and the Other Side of Globalization*. Bloomington, IN: Indiana University Press.

Scott, James. 1977. "Patronage or Exploitation?" In *Patrons and Clients in Mediterranean Societies*, edited by Ernest Gellner and John Waterbury, 21–40. London: Gerald Duckworth & Company Limited.

Seidman, Irving. 1998. *Interviewing as Qualitative Research: A Guide for Researchers in Education and the Social Sciences*. 2nd ed. New York, NY: Teachers College Press.

Sen, Amartya. 1999. *Development as Freedom*. London: Oxford University Press.

Singham, Archie W. 1968. *The Hero and the Crowd in a Colonial Polity*. New Haven, CT: Yale University Press.

Sirianni, Carmen. 2009. *Investing in Democracy: Engaging Citizens in Collaborative Governance*. Washington, DC: Brookings Institution Press.

Sives, Amanda. 1998. "Violence and Politics in Jamaica: An Analysis of Urban Violence in Kingston, 1944–1996." Doctoral Dissertation, University of Bradford.

———. 2002. "Changing Patrons, from Politician to Drug Don: Clientelism in Downtown Kingston, Jamaica." *Latin American Perspectives* 29 (5): 66–89.

———. 2010. *Elections, Violence and the Democratic Process in Jamaica 1944–2007*. Kingston, Jamaica: Ian Randle Publishers.

Social Development Commission (SDC), United Nations Development Program (UNDP) and Jamaica Violence Prevention Program. Brown Villa* Community Profile. 2011. SDC & UNDP.

Stivers, Camilla. 2008. *Governance in Dark Times: Practical Philosophy for Public Service*. Washington, DC: Georgetown University Press.

Stone, Carl. 1972. "Social Class and Partisan Attitudes in Urban Jamaica." *Social & Economic Studies* 21 (1): 1–29.

———. 1976. "Class and the Institutionalization of Two-party Politics in Jamaica." *Journal of Commonwealth and Comparative Politics* 14 (2): 177–96.

———. 1980. *Democracy and Clientelism in Jamaica*. University of the West Indies, Mona: Institute of Social and Economic Research.

———. 1985. *Democracy and Clientelism in Jamaica*. 3rd ed. New Brunswick, NJ: Transaction Books.

———. 1986. *Class, State, and Democracy in Jamaica*. New York, NY: Praeger.

———. 1986. *Power in the Caribbean Basin: A Comparative Study of Political Economy*. Philadelphia, PA: Institute for the Study of Human Issues.

———. 1989. *Carl Stone on Jamaican Politics, Economics and Society*. Kingston, Jamaica: Gleaner Co.

———, and University of the West Indies (Mona, Jamaica). 1973. *Class, Race, and Political Behaviour in Urban Jamaica*. Mona, Jamaica: Institute of Social and Economic Research, University of the West Indies.

Strange, Susan. 1996. *The Retreat of the State: The Diffusion of Power in the World Economy*. New York, NY: Cambridge University Press.

———, Peter B. Evans, Dietrich Rueschemeyer, and Theda Skocpol. 1985. *War Making and State Making as Organized Crime*. Cambridge: Cambridge University Press.

Tulchin, Joseph S., and Ralph H. Espach. 2000. *Security in the Caribbean Basin: The Challenge of Regional Cooperation*. Boulder, CO: L. Rienner.

United Nations Office on Drugs and Crime (UNODC). 2008. *World Drug Report 2008*. New York, NY: United Nations.

———. 2009. *World Drug Report 2009*. New York, NY: United Nations.

———. 2010. *World Drug Report 2010*. New York, NY: United Nations.

Vigil, James Diego. 2003. "Urban Violence and Street Gangs." *Annual Review of Anthropology* 32, 225–42.

Volkov, Vadim. 2002. *Violent Entrepreneurs: The Use of Force in the Making of Russian Capitalism*. Ithaca, NY: Cornell University Press.

———. 1996. *Drugs in the Western Hemisphere: An Odyssey of Cultures in Conflict*. Wilmington, DE: Scholarly Resources.

Warmington-Granston, Nicole, and Damion Blake. 2020. "State-Building in the Anglo-Caribbean: Assessing Jamaica's State Formation and Development." *Journal of Global South Studies* 37 (1): 110–38.

Weber, Max. 1978. *Economy, and Society: An Outline of Interpretive Sociology*. Berkeley, CA: University of California Press.

———, Hans Heinrich Gerth, Charles Wright Mills. 1991. *From Max Weber: Essays in Sociology*. London: Routledge.

Witter, W. 1992. "Patron Clientelism: Implications for Garrison Communities." Paper Presented at the Symposium, Grassroots Development, and the State of the Nation, 16–17. University of the West Indies, Mona, Jamaica,

Wolcott, Harry F. 1994. *Transforming Qualitative Data: Description, Analysis, and Interpretation*. Thousand Oaks, CA: Sage Publications.

Wolfgang, Marvin, and Franco Ferracuti. 1967. *The Subculture of Violence*. London: Tavistock.

Woody, C. 2018. "These Were the 50 Most Violent Cities in the World." *Business Insider*, March 6. Retrieved from https://www.businessinsider.com/most-violent-cities-in-the-world-2018-3.

World Bank. 2011. *Jamaica: Country Economic Memorandum: Unlocking Growth*. Washington, DC: World Bank.

Wrong, Dennis H. 1994. *The Problem of Order: What Unites and Divides Society*. New York, NY: The Free Press.

Youngers, Coletta, and Eileen Rosin. 2005. *Drugs and Democracy in Latin America: The Impact of U.S. Policy*. Boulder, CO: L. Rienner.

Young, Jock. 1999. *The Exclusive Society: Social Exclusion, Crime and Difference in Late Modernity*. London: Sage.

Young, Oran. 1999. *Governance in World Affairs*. Ithaca, NY: Cornell University Press.

Index

www.ingramcontent.com/pod-product-compliance
Lightning Source LLC
Chambersburg PA
CBHW031137270326
41929CB00011B/1657